AMERICA'S SMALL HOUSES

AMERICA'S SMALL HOUSES

(and City Apartments)

The Personal Homes of Designers and Collectors

By Henry Lionel Williams and Ottalie K. Williams

With an Introduction by J. A. Lloyd Hyde

BONANZA BOOKS · NEW YORK

© MCMLXIV by A. S. Barnes and Co., Inc.
Library of Congress Catalogue Card Number: 64-21363

This edition published by BONANZA BOOKS
a division of Crown Publishers, Inc.,
by arrangement with A. S. BARNES and Co., Inc.

Printed in the United States of America

Contents

II

CITY APARTMENTS

INTRODUCTION
Creative Beauty in Everyday Living

The avowed purpose of this book is to open up for the reader's delectation and profit some of the country's most attractive and original homes—both houses and apartments—owned by people of taste and distinction who have more than a passing interest in antiquities and other works of art and craftsmanship, and their place in everyday living. These are the professional antiquarians, the interior designers and architects, the collectors and connoisseurs who, in pursuit of the beautiful and enchanting (so often also the unique and priceless!), have found the means of surrounding themselves with an atmosphere of grace and charm in the midst of which mere existence becomes a joy, adapting their most treasured possessions—whether a few pieces or an extensive collection—to their everyday living, without the sacrifice of the amenities or loss of interest and comfort in their domiciles.

Here we see the results of disciplined imagination combined with cultivated knowledge in providing original solutions to the basic problems of contriving intimate backgrounds for living; we become acquainted with highly diversified interiors, free of vulgar ostentation, revealing the varied yet always discriminating tastes of gifted people whose creative ideas can be highly stimulating to others faced with similar problems of expression—ideas that often can be adapted to the needs and circumstances of individuals with like aspirations but differing experience and resources. These examples illustrate principles essential to success in a variety of situations, often emphasizing the spice of the unexpected which can transform the humdrum into the exciting. They demonstrate the value of combining the exotic and the familiar (mixing antique sculpture with modern painting, for example); of choosing antiques that have something beside mere age to recommend them. Even the practicality of designing simple houses is touched upon—houses with high ceilings and ample wall space to accommodate treasures unsuited to average rooms, at the same time providing them with ancient or modern architectural settings suited to the desired overall character of the interiors.

In these pages the Williamses have confined their attention to a score of individual homes in the Eastern States, and it is expected that future volumes will present equally interesting examples from other parts of the country, revealing in greater detail not only the vast and varied treasures to be found in this fabulous land of ours, but the ever-widening interest of those of means and taste in making such examples of creative beauty a part of their everyday living while preserving them for future generations to enjoy.

J. A. Lloyd Hyde

New York, 1964

7

I

Country and Town Houses

THE COUNTING HOUSE

The Home of Gardiner E. Somarindyck, Antiquarian

12

STONE ROOM
In the Stone Room furniture is limited to provide space for informal gatherings.
The floor remains unadorned by rugs.

The transformation of an eighteenth century counting house into a comfortable and elegant home agreeably furnished with high grade antiques calls for a high degree of imagination and no little taste. Friends who learned of Mr. Somarindyck's plans for such a tour de force a few years ago were more than a little intrigued at the possibilities—or lack of them. Apart from the limitations of the building itself there were problems of accessibility because of the steep hillside on which it was perched, and of interior arrangement due to the necessary location of the exterior doors, two walls of the high basement being totally exposed.

All of these apparent drawbacks have, surprisingly enough, been turned into assets, and today the two-story-and-basement, barnlike structure, with its beautifully proportioned gambrel roof, is the envy of the skeptics and the delight of connoisseurs—besides

13

DRAWING ROOM
Furnished in the manner of the owner's Paris apartment, the Drawing Room
strikes a novel note with its New England beamed ceiling and fireplace paneling.

being totally unlike any run-of-the-mill conversion that could have been expected. The new owner, however, had four things in his favor: a knowledge of old furniture, exquisite taste, a penchant for individuality, and a determination to make the most of a fascinating historical structure whose principal asset was a perfect location high on a bank overlooking the Connecticut River.

After many years as a buyer of antiques in Europe, Mr. Somarindyck was forced to vacate his Paris apartment when France was occupied by the invading German armies. Some of his antiques had been hurriedly shipped home to the United States, others were crated and sent for safety to his house in the country, twenty-odd miles from Paris. By the war's end most of the furniture in France had disappeared, and one of the few salvaged antiques was found in the rubbish dump of a cottage on the country property.

On Somarindyck's return to America it took many

DRAWING ROOM

A magnificent Louis XV marquetry commode is the *pièce de résistance* of the Counting House Drawing Room, companion piece to a secrètaire once owned by Colette.

months of searching before he discovered the old time structure that was to become his new home—a counting house once owned by Governor John Trumbull whose ships tied up at a nearby wharf. In later years it had been used for storage, and was finally allowed to lie fallow as an interesting 18th century survival that no one could find a use for. Although its interior has now been greatly remodeled, it still retains the external characteristics that betray its origins, with its stone walled basement, its solid shutters locked by bolts through the oak frames; its bar locked doors, and a side entrance at main floor level with a tiny balcony replacing the steps that led to the ground. Its massive gables have twin overhangs, with a pair of windows to each end of the attic space, and the rear wall supported by a thick

DINING ROOM

**Small, but impressive, the Dining Room combines French and Dutch pieces of
similar style with English oak, relying for color on a large Beauvais tapestry.**

stone foundation half buried in the hillside where a
new door, atop this wall, gives access to the garden.
Of necessity the principal entrance had to be re-
tained in the gable end where it opens on to a steep
hillside road, thus determining the floor plan to a
large degree.

In remodeling the building to serve as a house, as
much as possible of the original structure was preserved, including the old timbers and the naked ceiling joists and beams, the rear retaining wall that presents a rough granite face rising four feet above the

floor of what has, in consequence, come to be known
as The Stone Room. An original corner fireplace in
the new Drawing Room, with its fielded panels, was
saved, and another fireplace built to back it up in the
Stone Room, at right angles to a new and very large,
small paned, sliding triple window overlooking the
river. Off the Drawing Room a new stairway was installed, leading to the upper floor. Two bathrooms,
a powder room, and a kitchen were tucked away in
odd corners and, in each room, upstairs and down,
the walls were finished in wood or plaster to form the

16

DINING ROOM
**A monastic note set by the rough trestle table is counteracted by elegant seated
pieces and crimson floor length draperies.**

required background against which the various furnishings could be displayed to the best advantage.

In this manner it was possible to organize the space both conveniently and economically, with the tiny kitchen opening off the small entrance hall where it faces the Dining Room, and a short passage leads to the Stone Room. The large, many windowed Drawing Room opens off both the Dining Room and the Stone Room. Upstairs are the Morning Room, two Bedrooms and the two Bathrooms, all arranged around a large and airy stair landing. So compact is

this grouping that the house, though small enough to simplify living for one person, is pleasantly adaptable for entertaining on a moderate scale.

Because of the unusual though decidedly trim exterior, one gets the impression, on approaching the house, that this is something different. Therefore, on entering, one is not too surprised at the novel arrangement of the rooms, a striking feature being the extra large doorways which emphasize the circulation possibilities of air and light and add to the feeling of roominess and welcome. In addition, the colors

STONE ROOM

The Stone Room gets its name from the stone wall necessitated by the hillside
foundation which is made an attractive feature.

and textures of the walls and draperies, the furnishings and wood tones, contribute an air of warmth and ease, while the plain backgrounds, and the rigid lines of the structural elements provide the necessary contrast so that the furniture pieces stand out as units eliminating any suggestion of clutter. In addition they supply a note of austerity that emphasizes the beauty of line, pattern, and color of furniture and furnishings.

Though most of the furniture is of French origin, the rooms are not conceived in terms of a single style. Of the three main floor rooms, the Stone Room is probably the most used and the least formal—a feeling emphasized by the pine shelf capping the stone wall as a base for the wide, feather edged boarding of the upper wall. The walls are covered with sheathing of three different varieties of wood (the oak floor adds a fourth), with panels under the low window bottom and forming the doors of the built-in cupboard alongside the fireplace. The ceiling is off white plaster, centrally divided by the main beam, and, in one corner, steps lead up to the Dutch door opening on to the garden.

In keeping with the owner's philosophy of making

MORNING ROOM

A feature of the second floor Morning Room is this exquisite grouping of hanging vitrine and *dos d'âne* desk.

the most of each room element, the wood tones and interesting grain of the random-width flooring are not hidden by rugs. In addition, the room is sparsely furnished to leave ample floor space for those informal gatherings where people circulate (often glass in hand) while providing at other times for cosy conversational groups around the fireplace or at the window with its everchanging panorama of water, woods and sky. This window, and the two short ones above the wall, are adorned with flowered chintz draperies, the open floral pattern of soft pink and blue green on a two toned beige background, are edged with dark beige tassels, the essence of dignified informality.

In this mellow setting the most conspicuous piece of furniture—and the most cherished—is an 18th century French Provincial *bureau-plat* of unusual design, the rounded outer corners of the legs finished with the same narrow lip molding as the apron, the legs themselves curving inward at the bottom and ending in a square pad foot. The single drawer is lipped and decorated with shallow carving. Most extraordinary, however, is the dropped apron at the rear, the scalloped drop nicely carved in a floral design. On the wall ledge above this is another personal treasure—a set of five Creil faïence plates in polychrome depicting hunting scenes which add a dash of color. This grouping is topped off by one of a pair of massive Flemish or Dutch three branch sconces in brass, now inconspicuously electrified, on the wall above them.

The seating pieces are confined to a huge Louis XIV *bergère* in gold brocade, an American straight legged corner chair with pierced splats, a pair of small, cane-seated Pennsylvania Dutch side chairs and a Martha Washington chair in gold, hand blocked linen. In the narrow wall space between the powder room door and the hall passage, is a tall 18th century armoire in carved fruitwood. It has huge ball feet, glass in the upper door panel, and long decorative hinges in gilt bronze. It was probably intended for hat storage, and is striking enough to decorate the entire room end.

Among the metal accessories and bibelots are pieces of brass, copper, and pewter ware, augmented by a Dutch style, six branch ball type brass chandelier. The brass andirons are of Régence style, each consisting of an attenuated dolphin spiralling around a vertical trident. A bail handled and footed copper pail carries a crest in relief on one side and a *fleur de lis* on the other, while a smaller, but somewhat similar, piece in copper and brass is given a crown shape

by heavy wire loops around the top terminating in a ball finial. Its small opening suggests that it might have been a pastille burner.

In elaborate contrast with the Stone Room is the Louis XV Drawing Room whose splendid French antiques seem quite at home with the discolored ceiling beams, the wide plank floor and undraped windows. The colors are enchanting, from the delicate pale green of the walls to the gold and plum of the upholstery and the gleaming, varnished dark *acajou* and kingwood of a magnificent Louis XV marquetry commode. Although but three drawers high, this piece actually has four drawers, one side of the top section being longer than the other by the width of the flat central portion. Its brown marble top is flecked in black and white, the body ornamented with ormolu *chutes* and *sabots,* drop handles and escutcheons. The beautiful creation which, like the rest of the important pieces, came from the owner's Paris apartment, has the further distinction of being companion piece to a *secrétaire* once owned by the famed Colette. Since neither she nor Mr. Somarindyck would part with their half of the set the two were never reunited.

On this commode is another of the room's unusual items, a late 18th century French clock with a deeply etched glass dial, delicate brass hands, and an ormolu mounted double marble base. Even the casing over the works is beautifully chased. The commode itself is given considerable added importance in this high ceilinged room by a wide pier glass with a gilt gesso frame, its elaborate cresting reaching almost to the frieze. Mirrors are, as a matter of fact, an important feature of this room. Bevelled glasses at each end, with Baccarat crystal appliqués centered in them, reflect one another and enough room detail to add sparkle and interest. Placed over furniture pieces they add to the visual height, and balance a French brocade hanging alongside the fireplace.

Under one of these mirrors is an Italian three drawer marquetry commode on which stands an especially fine piece of statuary in *blanc de Chine.* There are several other marquetry tables and stands dispersed among the seated pieces, including a three drawer card table whose folding top is lined with felt, and a Louis XV coffee table which can be extended by two pull-out leaves. The largest of the furniture pieces is a particularly handsome Louis XV *canapé à corbeille* upholstered in plum colored wool mohair, the beechwood frame in its natural light color. In this group are fauteuils and bergères in gold

BEDROOM

A bedroom eye catcher is the early 18th century carved and pierced bed, baroque in style, wryly contrasting with the burl-walnut *poudreuse* of the same period.

brocade which matches the loose cushions of a pair of cane-backed Régence armchairs. Two early 18th century Italian high cane-back side chairs are included for contrast.

The corner fireplace wall supplies architectural interest with its Early American raised paneling separated only by molding from the surround of marbleized delft tiles with overall *aubergine* markings on a white ground. Next to it, on one of the small tables, stands a *bouillotte* lamp with a tôle shade. Four strongly patterned oriental rugs scattered about the floor not only supply a counterpoint of gay color but constitute a gesture toward quietude—and spike heels!

The Somarindyck Dining Room is small but impressive, with monastic overtones due largely to the simplicity of the rough trestle table, the bare pine floor, dead white walls and the exposed ceiling timbers between which the white painted undersides of the upper floor boards are seen. Adding to this atmosphere are the chandelier of turned wood and wire, and four Portuguese tôle sconces painted off white with pale blue borders. The room's wood trim, including a molded chair rail, is in natural finish, and the doors are given an air of solidity by the application of large raised panels above and below the lock rail.

This general impression of austerity is softened

somewhat by the floor length window draperies of a warm crimson fabric with pleated valances, and by the large and colorful Beauvais tapestry in beige and blue green, with touches of pink and blue, which covers most of one wall above an early English dark oak sideboard or dresser dated before 1700. Along the narrow (16 inch) top of the dresser are spaced four tall and dramatic silver candlesticks with large-diameter disk bases, twin spiral stems, and cut-glass bobêches. These are careful reproductions of originals belonging to a friend of the owner and are thought to be English.

Another notable feature of this small room is the manner in which various furniture styles have been combined into a harmonious whole. Two of the larger pieces—plus a large commode and tall marquetry cabinet—are French Provincial of the Louis XV period, and a pair of cane-back chairs are Dutch interpretations of the same style. The commode has two drawers whose fronts, as well as the side panels, are beautifully carved in relief. It is also distinguished by small *pieds de biche* in front, and unusually handsome hardware. The cabinet—really a tall, slender vitrine—has a carved and decorated panel below, and corners inlaid with an undulating line in tulipwood. Its three shelves displaying Export China are visible through the upper glass door which occupies about two thirds of the cabinet's height.

The room seating includes Louis XIV carved armchairs with cane backs and seats, and a pair of rush-seated 18th century Italian dining chairs with cushions of crimson damask. The cottage style table is Early American, completing an altogether interesting and somewhat exotic mélange of pieces which give the room a special character that could not have been achieved by adhering strictly to any one period or style or formal background and decoration.

Upstairs there are several items of special interest, such as an early 18th century Italian bed, carved and pierced in riotous abandon that even John Henry Belter would have envied—yet a noble piece, the epitome of 17th-century baroque which stands out from the plain and demure pieces with which it is surrounded. These latter consist of one- and three-drawer inlaid night tables, and 18th century Italian burl-walnut poudreuse which has a compelling charm that its decorative set of china toilet and pomade jars by no means diminishes. Opposite this stands a very tall Louis XVI chest in marquetry with a marble top that one would need steps to examine.

Next door, in the Morning Room, is an exquisite group composed of the inlaid fruitwood French Provincial *dos d'âne* desk with a leather padded drop-front, previously mentioned as having been rescued from a wartime trash heap; a Louis XV stool below it upholstered in its original red cut-velvet, and, above these, a delicately framed vitrine with its original glass, displaying bibelots including colorful and rare china cups and saucers, enameled watch dials, a fan, and a collection of tiny figurines.

The rest of the rooms follow the same pattern, mixing Italian and French pieces of the late 17th and early 18th centuries against varying backgrounds of beiges, pinks and blues, pattern being confined to draperies, with rugs of soft, receding colors or none at all, so as not to overwhelm the furniture, every piece of which is lovely enough to stand alone.

PARSNIP HOLLOW

The Country Home of Amos W. Shepard, Antiquarian

26

DINING ROOM

Furnished as of 1740, the Dining Room pieces are of American and English origin in pine, chestnut, maple and oak with a profusion of rush seats and primitive colors.

The old time center chimney New England house that antiquarian Amos Shepard restored to serve as his country home was built in 1795, and a wing was added in 1810. It has ceilings and walls of rough plaster, dado high wainscoting, cased corner posts, floors of chestnut planks, and raised panel doors, with old-time cornice moldings and paneled fireplace walls in the more formal rooms. These, together with the small paned windows, create the nostalgic atmos-phere in which his pine, walnut, and mahogany pieces, ranging in age from the 17th to the 19th century, seem equally at home in rooms arranged to represent either some specific period or more than 200 years of development and change.

On the main floor, for example, the Dining Room is furnished as of 1740 with American and English antiques, as is another one which is called the Chinese Room because of its oriental wallpaper. The

DINING ROOM
The subdued colors of the Dining Room are enlivened by draperies of eggplant,
blue, and burgundy and an antique oriental rug repeating these hues.

Living Room, on the other hand, is furnished purely for comfort and convenience with 17th and 18th century pieces, while the Parlor is dedicated to Sheraton style antiques of the mid-1700s or thereabouts.

In spite of this variation in period, each room has something in common with the rest, even if it be only the background of *boiserie* and trim, so that there is a certain unity of feeling throughout the house. This makes for smoothness of transition from one area to another without detracting from the individuality or interest of any of the rooms. Furthermore, a convincing air of antiquity has been recaptured in what is actually a highly livable home in the modern sense without the overall colonial atmosphere degenerating into that of a museum. One reason for this is the fact that the furniture and accessories have been selected with care. All of them are of excellent quality, and the mistake has not been made of mixing home made country pieces with those of authentic design and skilled craftsmanship; the kitchen pieces, in other words, have been confined to the kitchen.

28

LIVING ROOM

A sober color scheme ties together the varying styles of furniture in the Living Room, the walls being a soft mustard, the trim a yellowish green.

Even in the long, L-shaped Living Room (formerly the Keeping Room plus a small added ell) where no attempt was made to keep every item in period, the styles may vary but the quality is consistent, and all is tied together by a sober color scheme in which violent tones have been avoided. The off white ceiling helps reflect the light from four windows, two of which face the fireplace. The plaster walls are finished in a soft mustard tone, while the mantel, wainscoting and trim are painted a yellowish green. In contrast, the floor, which is largely hidden by oriental rugs in muted tones, is finely spattered in several colors over a brick red ground. These colors are repeated in the sill long curtains of heavy silk which tone in nicely with the soft brown and deep red of an early 19th century sofa.

At each end of the room is a furniture piece of major interest, one being a 17th century oak and pine, four drawer chest of New England origin with bun feet, four drawers with heavy moldings dividing each drawer front into two panels, and original brass

29

LIVING ROOM
Featured at this end of the Living Room is a 17th century ten-sided table on a
triangular base with a melon turned gate-leg.

lock escutcheons. The other is an equally rare duo-decagonal table of about the same period. This has a triangular base with a marbleized folding top, and three black painted, melon turned legs, one of which is split to form a gate. The scalloped apron is quite deep, and painted a dull red with black bands. Though it is probably of Scandinavian origin, dating from around 1650, there is one from Essex, Massachusetts, almost duplicating it, in New York's Metropolitan Museum.

Another rare piece in this room is a 17th century American turned joint stool with vertical legs and flame stitch upholstery. Where the room turns at ninety degrees to form a bookcase lined entrance hall there is a painted, built-in corner cupboard. Its double doors and open shelves display some interesting pieces of English delft ware. Two other features of note are a pair of lifelike carved ducks in

wood, hailing from France, which grace the old table, and an American primitive painting hung over the aforementioned New England chest.

The little Sheraton Parlor reflects the surprisingly sophisticated taste occasionally encountered in early 19th century New England homes. Here, lilac gray walls and somewhat darker trim set off to perfection certain fancy Sheraton pieces painted in red and gold. Normally, this room is flooded with daylight through three large windows which a room sized 1815 Aubusson rug does little to diminish, thanks to its light gold ground and wide scattering of flowers in pink and green. Equally reflective are the highly stylized pink cotton curtains topped by stunning floral prints on a grayish mauve background that form the triple swags of handsome pelmets printed in claret and gray.

The furniture pieces consist of an eight legged

LIVING ROOM
At each end of the Living Room is a furniture piece of major interest—this one
being a 17th century oak and pine New England chest with bun feet.

American fancy Sheraton settee with a caned seat and diamond shaped back panels, plus a pair of matching arm chairs, an arch centered desk in red and gold with six simulated bamboo legs and five drawers, and a matching chair with a rush seat. Between two windows is a large and handsome, flat topped English tall clock in mahogany whose dial indicates the seasons. Another accent is provided by an octagonal tripod birdcage table in black lacquer with gold decoration; a nest of Chinese tables in red, black, and gold, and a delicate pair of shield shaped pole screens alongside the fireplace, painted in red, gold, and green on a neutral ground, while over the mantel hangs a gilt framed bull's-eye mirror.

Other appointments and the mantel garniture are in period, the cachepots and decorative animals being of Chinese Export porcelain, details that make this the most carefully decorated room in the house,

even to the amethyst globes on silver plated light fixtures which flank an early 18th century gold framed portrait over the desk.

The Chinese Room is a definitely American 1740 parlor with a distinctly oriental flavor, and every bit as attractive as the Sheraton Room though much more exotic in style. The fine Chinese wallpaper— painted in China about 1740—is the most attractive feature of the room, and certainly the most striking. It was found on the walls of a house near Versailles (France), and the warm tone given to the very fine dado paneling beneath it reproduces one of its predominant colors. Similar raised paneling, painted a creamy beige also forms the fireplace overmantel, and below this the fireplace surround has some particularly fine bolection molding. The dado cap also is nicely molded in the 18th century manner, as are the window frames, an elaboration that renders them all

31

LIVING ROOM
Another view of the melon turned table, showing the folding marbleized top
and scalloped apron. Probably Scandinavian of around 1650.

the more in keeping with the highly decorative pelmets which once formed part of an ecclesiastical vestment. These are of gold colored, watered silk with green and taupe trim and gold tassels.

Peculiarly suited to this room is the high backed Chippendale settee, originating in Edinburgh, which is upholstered in crewel work of tones compatible with those of the paper and the interior woodwork. This stands on a large Feraghan rug whose tiny floral pattern picks up the coral pink, blue, and green accents of the wallpaper. The rug's most prevalent

tint of pink is repeated in a pair of Chippendale straight legged chairs whose seats and backs are upholstered in a coral pink velvet. Separated by the width of the room, these provide striking accents where they are most effective.

One of the finest pieces of furniture in the room is a rare japanned tea table of Chinese pattern, dating from 1790. Another important antique is a round American tripod table in walnut with a birdcage top and an unusually shapely and substantial pedestal turning. A duplicate of this is to be found in the Van

Salon in the penthouse of Churchill J. Brazelton. (See page 233)

Drawing room in the country residence of George W. Helm, Jr., and George Hickey III. (See page 81)

The principal bedroom in the residence of Jerome Zerbe. (See page 49)

Living room in the seashore residence of George H. Clark. (See page 151)

The library of Clifton, the plantation residence of Harry T. Peters, Jr. (See page 91)

Entrance hall of the country-village house of Mrs. Truman P. Handy. (See page 39)

Living room in Parsnip Hollow, the country home of Amos W. Shepard. (See page 25)

The library of Brickhouse Farm, residence of Mr. and Mrs. Kenneth Chorley.
(See page 61)

Reception room in Longue Vue, the residence of Mrs. Edgar B. Stern. (See page 121)

The salon of the Zerbe residence. (See page 49)

Drawing room in Le Marais, home of Mrs. Wylie Brown. (See page 131)

Drawing room in the home of Gardiner E. Somarindyck. (See page 11)

The drawing room of Hopedene, summer home of Mr. and Mrs. Charles C. Paterson. (See page 107)

Bedroom in Stoke Poges, country residence of Mrs. John Wintersteen. (See page 141)

Library in the town apartment of Mr. and Mrs. Harold W. Carhart. (See page 225)

The entrance hall to the Peters residence, Clifton. (See page 91)

Den in the town apartment of Elmo D. Avet. (See page 243)

Dining room of the summer home of Mr. and Mrs. Charles C. Paterson. (See page 107)

Salon of the Michael Greer apartment. (See page 203)

Salon in the town apartment of J. A. Lloyd Hyde. (See page 217)

Drawing room of the farmhouse of Mr. and Mrs. J. Liddon Pennock. (See page 71)

Dining room in the town house of Mr. and Mrs. David Stockwell. (See page 177)

Oriental room in the converted mill residence of R. Hatfield Ellsworth. (See page 165)

Dining room of Parsnip Hollow, the Shepard country home. (See page 25)

SHERATON PARLOR
A sophisticated Sheraton Parlor with lilac walls and fancy Sheraton pieces in red
and gold on an Aubusson rug of gold with pink and green flowers.

Cortlandt Manor House on the Hudson. There is also a rare hexagonal candlestand with a raised gallery upheld by a ring of tiny turned balusters. The only other important piece here is a cane-backed early 18th century American armchair, but over the fireplace is an unusually interesting group composed of an English Chippendale mirror in a gilt frame, carved in a shell motif with volutes which is repeated in the pair of wall sconces flanking it.

The Dining Room is one of the most inviting rooms in the house, a room completely integrated and balanced, furnished in the 1740 period with substantial American and English pieces in the usual pine, chestnut, maple, and oak, with a profusion of rush seats, wood paneling, and primitive colors, all reminiscent of colonial days. This room extends the full depth of the house, and one striking innovation is a huge bow window with small panes which takes up most of one end wall and, by daytime, floods the room with light. This provides it with a fascinating focal point, bringing it to life as nothing else could except, perhaps, a fire in the hearth.

33

SHERATON PARLOR
Featured in the Sheraton Parlor is a flat topped English tall clock in mahogany.

The room is long and only moderately wide, with two windows at the opposite end to the bay. Its walls and ceilings are an off white suggestive of oyster shell lime, the wainscot, trim, chair-rail, moldings and window woodwork a subdued gray green, splashes of color being introduced by draperies of an antique India print in eggplant, blue, and burgundy on a beige ground. Several of these colors are repeated in the antique oriental rug which extends beyond the table ends. In front of the great fireplace is a massive chestnut dining table (circa 1720) which has a top two inches thick and unusual, eared trestles. Around it are arranged banister back chairs with loose cushions in deep burgundy. Two other fine pieces are a 17th century English japanned highboy with sausage turned legs and carved stretcher, on which are displayed a pair of porcelain ducks and a colorful Lowestoft bowl, and a walnut Queen Anne dresser.

CHINESE ROOM

The Chinese Room is a 1740 American Parlor with an oriental flavor. Its outstanding feature a Chinese wallpaper of 1740 found in France. The pelmets are gold watered silk once part of ecclesiastical vestments.

The dresser is quite imposing with its inlaid drawers and trumpet-turned legs with ball feet. This is adorned with a shagreen knife-box containing a collection of English cutlery, and a pair of Queen Anne silver candleholders. Across the room from this is another English dresser of carved oak whose legs and stretcher incorporate sausage turnings. Flanking the fireplace are a pair of Connecticut winged and scalloped hanging shelves displaying a collection of pewter and delft ware. Here, as elsewhere throughout the house, the lighting fixtures have been electrified and equipped with "candylbeme" bulbs whose tiny yellow "flame" does much to add to the homelike feel and antique air of the interiors after dark.

THE COUNTRY-VILLAGE HOUSE OF

Mrs. Truman P. Handy, Interior Designer

STAIR HALL

This Side Hall accommodates a painted console table, a tall clock with wooden works, a highback chair and an English needlework rug against the background of a decorative stair with life size pineapple finials.

The interiors of few small town houses lend themselves so well to the adequate placing of furniture, or provide so many fascinating vistas as Charlotte Handy's 1890 mansion in Connecticut. Immediately on entering, the visitor is faced with expansive views down the wide Hall which is separated only by a pair of classical columns from the Drawing Room and Stair Hall. Thanks to large windows and much white paint, the whole interior seems light and airy, unified by a vast expanse of shining, antique parquet floor which forms a rich background for brightly colored rugs with a formal air. Here and there are exquisite furniture pieces, tubs of flowering plants and everywhere masses of seasonal blooms. Viewed from the Hall, the whole has an air of splendid variety, warranted to arouse curiosity as to the source of its overall undeniable charm.

The house itself is substantial Victorian with white

HALL

Tall white columns and a gold needlework rug set a formal note for the Hall which houses collectors' pieces from a huge Italian table to carved Flemish cane back chairs.

UPPER HALL

White swagged draperies over the triple window and a gold pattern on white wallpaper set off a crystal adorned bucket style lantern centered over the stair well in the Upper Hall.

DRAWING ROOM

This side of the oval Drawing Room derives its character from the statuary niches and paneling augmented by floor length curtains in white silk damask.

painted clapboards, large windows, and a pair of semicircular pillared porches projecting so provocatively from the east façade as to suggest to one admiring visitor that they called for a snug brassiere! Nevertheless, the whole three story structure is stately and reserved, with a dignified entrance under the front porch, set off by fluted Roman-Doric columns. The colored glass of the front door has been replaced by clear bevelled panes restoring the chaste appearance of the classical Hall inside as well as the entrance exterior.

The Hall itself is wide enough to afford space for adequate furnishing, and long enough to demand a formal arrangement to balance the columns to one side. These things it has. Down the center is one long rug of English needlework in gold, with a pattern of scattered leaves in white, suggesting carefully spaced *fleurs de lis,* inside a white border with black edging. To one side is a huge Italian table with a top grained in browns, its square, recessed tapering legs and the scalloped apron painted a soft green. Behind this is a floor length mirror reflecting the massive

44

DRAWING ROOM

The Drawing Room furniture is an attractive mixture of Italian, French, and English pieces, principally in gold and white with red accents. Note the bird pictures which are still fascinating without their feathers!

columns forming the Drawing Room entrance. On the wall at each side is an ormolu and crystal, four branch girandole, of which there are several others spaced along the hall.

Against the end wall, a pair of tall American Flemish cane-back, carved chairs with scroll feet and scarlet cushions—provenance Salem, Massachusetts—deflect one through a flat archway into the Stair Hall, past one Hall side chair of Queen Anne style with openwork splat and stretchers. In the Stair Hall itself

there is a tall backed bergère with the tiny wings that label it as French—another reminder of the things, individual and unusual, that endow this interior with its fascinating character.

The side hall, being almost square, can accommodate several pieces of furniture, including a massive painted console table with a bookshelf in the apron; a Connecticut tall clock with wooden works which is a family heirloom, and a high-back chair with a needlework seat in soft colors. The antique

45

PRINCIPAL BEDROOM
Backgrounds of the Principal Bedroom are gray paneling duplicating the
ground of the reproduction French wallpaper which carries a figure in orange
with touches of blue. Light blue taffeta swags are bordered in white, the blue
repeated in the chair cushions.

English needlework rug here is similar in pattern and
color to that of the Main Hall, but it has a wide floral
border in blue and old rose.

A great, arched triple window lights both upper
and lower Stair Halls and the stair itself. The highly
decorative staircase, which occupies the window
wall, has white painted panels, balusters, and newel
posts, with mahogany treads and handrail, the last
named embellished with life size pineapple finials.

The newels are swash turned, and the balusters sport
three differing styles of turnings to each step. Centered in front of the window, with its white swagged
draperies, gold cords, and topped by a gilded eagle in
the round, is a large, bucket-style lantern of glass
trimmed with crystals, and hung from gilded brass
hoops. The wallpaper here is a diaper pattern of *fleur
de lis* in gold on a white ground.

There is nothing Victorian about the Drawing

Room which has an Adam air, with a suggestion of the Federal, due to the oval shape and the large statuary niches with shell tops and fluted backs. These are occupied by Italian pedestals composed of figures sculptured in black basalt. There are three windows to the room, with floor length draperies in white silk damask which hang from poles above the trim. Between two of them is a long, marble topped Italian commode painted in two tones of green, and over this hangs an oval mirror, gilt-framed in the Adam style with an urn and flower cresting reaching almost to the ceiling.

At the fireplace end of the room the principal feature is a stripped mantel, quite French in feeling with its delicate carving in swags and pendants, and decorative touches even to the edge of the mantel shelf itself. This came from an old house in Massachusetts. As in the halls, the floor here is part of the same antique parquet, with a fine Aubusson rug concealing as little of its glossy surface as possible in the conversation area. Black bordered with a fine red line, the rug has a central medallion, with floral designs in light gray and red on a gold ground, confined to the corners. The furniture is an attractive mixture of Italian, French, and English pieces—cane-back fruitwood chairs with gold and white taffeta cushions and leather padded arms; a love-seat in white brocade; a small, painted, light gray chair and matching stool covered in gold with strawberry trim; a pair of Louis XV fauteuils upholstered in a red, green, and gold floral pattern on a white ground—the whole a triumph of eclectic selection and arrangement.

The recurrent white, incidentally, carries out the theme set by the white walls, columns and ceiling, the draperies, and other white accents supplied by china pieces and some of the pictures. An amusing note is struck by one set of bird pictures which originally had been given a lifelike touch by the application of real feathers to the bodies. Long afterwards a "restoration" had been carried out by transferring the feathers to new paintings. This left the bodies of the original birds as ghostly blank spaces on the white paper. The effect was both novel and startling,

and when Mrs. Handy had these originals framed in their denuded condition, the "plucked" watercolors gave the impression of a new and exciting art technique. Actually these pictures are quite attractive, and today seem fully at home with the mantel garniture of Chelsea and Whieldon chinaware. Over the mantel is a family portrait in oils, and small tables on either side support Italian lamps with turned, carved, and gilt wooden bases.

Novel decorating touches also are found in the principal bedroom where the ceiling is off white, the panelling of the fireplace wall a delicate gray. This gray duplicates that forming the background of a reproduction French wallpaper which carries a figure in orange with touches of dull blue. The rug is a short nap style in off white, and there is a white border to the light blue taffeta drapery swags, each held by three large gilt buttons. This blue is repeated in the taffeta chair cushions, with the pale green of a Directoire chair which has ram's head arms providing one of those small shocks of delighted surprise that the skilled decorator occasionally contrives. Lustrous, bright metal has its place here, too—the gilded country church candlestands that share the mantel with white glazed Staffordshire lambs; a pair of French twin-candle lamps on the French Provincial dressing chest, and that timepiece-de-luxe, a gilt *cartel* with enamelled face on the wall nearby, plus the lesser accent of the brass gallery around the marble top of a *bouillotte* table. Still another note is struck by a pair of rush-seated turned chairs from some small country church which now flank the fireplace, and occasionally give rise to arguments as to the significance of the flat top rail that crowns the back.

It is pieces like this that point up the fact that a medley of styles judiciously assembled, and tied together with well chosen backgrounds and colors, makes for rooms with individuality and a spirited atmosphere in which there is never need to hunt for a conversation piece. All of this has here been obviously achieved.

THE COUNTRY RESIDENCE OF

Jerome Zerbe, Connoisseur

SALON

The Zerbe Salon combines comfort with luxury to an unusual degree, its "Grinling Gibbons" swags, crystal bronze doré chandeliers and coromandel screen contrasting with the light tan ceiling and delicate green walls.

While he may have no particular passion for collecting specific *objets de vertu,* Mr. Jerome Zerbe is undoubtedly possessed of an urge to surround himself with things of beauty, so many of which he has acquired in his world travels. This is more or less obvious from the country retreat he designed, built, and furnished for himself some years ago on the Connecticut River—a pavilion of grace and dignity such as he describes in his book: *Les Pavillons Francaises*

—a place to entertain a few privileged guests; to use merely as an escape from the workaday world, or perhaps recuperate from a hurried trip to far places as is so often his lot.

In any event this house of few but large and high ceiled rooms was built on its own tiny peninsula, with an enviable view up-river and never a neighbor in sight. A single story residence, it is severely functional in style, based on an irregular floor plan, with

51

SALON

A feature of the Salon is a huge bay with an unobstructed view of the Connecticut River. Twin Louis XV sofas, back to back, permit enjoyment of this view or the fireside at will.

walls of whitewashed brick. Its windows are high, its chimneys square blocks, its roof's flatness relieved by corner urns.

The principal room occupies a huge bay, the main bedroom projecting beyond the entrance façade, its two windows provided with artistic balcony rails, and guarded by twin putti in marble on the lawn nearby. In contrast, a french window of the large bay opens on to a flagged terrace with terminal statuary —so-called sphinxes—in the form of lionesses couch-

ant, with heads and upper figures in Louis XV low necked garb, and the faces of saucy demoiselles. Beyond this is a roofed porch with sculptured pieces, and the whole is delightfully landscaped, one lawn sloping down to the river, others dotted with urns on pedestals, and terminating in four tall, classical columns (of somewhat exotic detail) reminiscent of ancient ruins amid crowding shrubbery alongside a pleached allée.

In such an impressive setting it is no surprise to

SALON

Another aspect of the Zerbe Salon that shows the great bronze-trimmed double doors of butternut opening into the Foyer. The inset bookcase beside the marbleized wood fireplace is copied from an original at Versailles.

find the house interiors luxurious though comfortable and definitely charming. Opening off the impressive Foyer, through double doors with bronze hardware, is the Salon. This room, flooded with light from its tall windows, is the acme of elegance, its ceiling a light tan, its walls a delicate green, the draperies and pelmets in plain chartreuse silk, and the rugs light and colorful 18th century Persian. The floor is of antique oak parquetry, dark with age but highly polished; the doors and other woodwork in glowing natural butternut and walnut—a perfect setting for the exquisite furniture and decorative details. From the ceiling center hangs a cut-glass, rock crystal, and bronze doré chandelier, reflected in a huge square overmantel mirror in a slender gilt frame. This modern mirror is given greater importance by the decorative carvings around it—pieces reminiscent of the work of Grinling Gibbons—twin cornucopia above, sheaves of fruit, flowers and foliage at the sides, all in the round. The mantel itself is of wood painted to

PRINCIPAL BEDROOM

Paneling from a famous New York house and a historic wallpaper from Peking form a lavish setting for a white mantel familiar to Marie Antoinette and a lavish bed in yellow brocade in the Principal Bedroom.

represent a rich, red, white veined marble, with sweeping curves, molded and carved, an exact copy of one in Madame du Barry's house at Versailles. At its center stands an 18th century bust of some distinguished unknown, and the garniture is comprised of an 18th century pair of Chinese crackle and blue porcelain beakers. On the hearth stands an elaborately sculptured pair of *chenets* in bronze doré, 18th century reproductions of firedogs made by Pierre Gouthiére for Madame du Barry's *pavillon* on Louveciennes and which now repose in the Louvre.

Adding to the interest of this room is the fact that the walls flanking the fireplace are set at an angle, making it octagonal. The wall to the right of the fireplace is almost totally occupied by a built-in bookcase crammed with limited editions, fine bindings and rare volumes in several languages on important examples of domestic architecture and fine furniture. To the left, double doors open into a dining room and a modern kitchen, the latter leading, in turn, to the porch.

This end of the room is a mass of color thanks to an

PRINCIPAL BEDROOM
Prominent decorative features of the Bedroom are Chinese figures in *papier mâché* and a pair of Louis XV *dessertes*. The door leads to the Small Library.

eight panel, door high coromandel screen in gold, red, black, and white. In front of it is a Louis XV *bureau-plat* in marquetry with ormolu decoration whose chief ornament is a 19th century reproduction of Augustin Pajou's famous bust of Madame du Barry now in the Louvre. Here also is a pair of Chinese vases converted into lamp bases (*quelle ignominie!*), and a fascinating couple of Siamese or Cambodian figurines in brass representing natives

riding water buffaloes. Other tables of interest include an 18th century French *trictrac* (backgammon) board, and a square of parquet from Versailles mounted to form a coffee table top. An attractive pair of lamps in the bay were made from figurines that once decorated a Renaissance Italian tall chest.

The problem of either facing the fireplace on cool evenings or enjoying the outdoor vista through the bay windows is neatly solved by placing two large

SMALL LIBRARY

Paneled in Swedish pine, the walls of the Small Library are innocent of paint. Italian 18th century round backed chairs, a Russell pastel and an oversize 19th century porcelain Kuan Yin flanked by exquisite cranes of the same period are of especial interest. The 16th century bronze lotus bell came from the ruined Shiba Park in Tokio.

Louis XV sofas back to back. These have fruitwood frames and are covered in a tomato-colored textured fabric. Other color accents are provided by Louis XV bergères in green velvet, and a *dossier-plat* in beige brocade.

In contrast with the Salon, the principal Bedroom is positively exotic, with its three pale blue paneled walls from the Vanderbilt House on 51st Street in New York, and recessed fireplace, its fourth wall

papered with romping simians, and a fantastic bed draped in golden yellow brocade. Both the wallpaper and the fireplace have stirring histories. The wallpaper actually was painted in Peking in 1946 from the photographs of a Japanese scroll now in a Boston museum. It was one of the treasures brought out of China on the last of General Chennault's planes as the communists took over the city. The carved white mantel is even more interesting historically, having

One of the Louis XV sphinxes ornamenting the flagged terrace.

been originally installed in the famous Desert de Retz, a *folie* outside Paris where it must have been a familiar sight to Marie Antoinette, Madame du Barry, and many other fascinating historical figures prior to the French Revolution.

The bed itself apparently has no history of note, fabulous as it appears in its heavy silken hangings of yellow brocade lined with blue silk—a vivid color matched by the bed itself and copied on the walls. Its tasseled cords pick up both the yellow and the blue. Of almost equal interest is a pair of Chinese figures in *papier-mâché*, brilliantly colored and delightfully modelled. These were possibly made in China for the

European trade, though one authority believes they were made in Venice where they were found. No one, however, seems to know why their heads were made to nod! They stand on a pair of Louis XVI *dessertes*.

The mantel garniture consists of two elegant pieces of Sceaux porcelain in white, lavender, and green, and a pair of small terracotta sphinxes with putti and garlands. Another piece of note is a 17th century Japanese carved wooden figure of Kuan Yin, the popular goddess of mercy.

The floor of this room is of antique parquet, and the windows are hung with floor length draperies,

they and their valances being of the same blue as the walls, with a white fringe and ball tasseled tie-backs. The fauteuils are Louis XVI, carved and painted, with the original upholstery in gold with a floral pattern, brass nailed. There is also a bergère in rich gold velvet, and a *prie-dieu* in striped blue and tan upholstery, plus a tea table, its top in the form of a red lacquer tray decorated in gold and black.

A somewhat more sober atmosphere is captured in the small library with its paneled Swedish pine walls innocent of paint from the William Astor house at Rhinebeck, though it contains one or two things of value. Of particular interest are two 18th century Italian round-backed chairs, beautifully carved and fitted with cane seats. Originally white and gold they had undergone a thorough *décapage* long before they were acquired by the present owner. There is also a Louis XV daybed, white painted and covered

with beige silk fastened with brass nails.

Two walnut commodes flank the doorway, both with bronze doré hardware and nicely carved. On the larger one the oversize garniture pieces consist of a large and gaily colored 19th century Chinese porcelain Kuan Yin, and a pair of exquisitely executed porcelain cranes of the same period. On the smaller commode is a 16th century Japanese lotus bell in bronze from the ruins of Shiba Park, Tokio. The only picture in the room is a pastel portrait by John Russell (1744-1806), a contemporary and friend of Sir Joshua Reynolds (1724-1792). Here, as in the other rooms, there are minor items of more or less interest, but sufficient have been noted to indicate that in this unusual residence each room has its own special mood and character, so that monotony is the one characteristic hardest to find, and its points of interest many faceted.

BRICKHOUSE FARM

The Country Residence of Mr. and Mrs. Kenneth Chorley, Collectors

62

DINING ROOM

In the Chorley Dining Room, smoky dark wood, polished pewter and English delftware in a setting of old pine floors, beams and oyster white ceiling constitutes a charming period piece.

Set in the midst of its rolling upland acres, the early 19th century red brick residence of Mr. and Mrs. Kenneth Chorley looks out upon its picturesque barns, stables, cartsheds and carriage house, and beyond them to distant vistas. The house itself has all the appeal of an old-time homestead together with a certain architectural distinction that sets it apart. Internally, it constitutes not only a pleasant and practical domicile, but also a satisfying background for the beautiful, rare, and precious objects the Chorleys have collected over the years.

One of the changes made to the step roofed building was to fill in an archway opening into a recessed entry with a floor length, round topped window. The effect of this was to add to the Dining Room a space framed off from it by heavy posts and beams. These offer little obstruction to the light from the new and existing windows so that some of the gloom is dis-

LIBRARY

Antique and Modern mix happily in this Library, where antique pine shelves
display 17th and 18th century delftware.

pelled. The floor here is of red brick, delineating a
space that could very well serve as a pleasant and
cosy nook for dining *à deux!*

The Dining Room itself is far different from most
of its kind, and actually one of the most enchanting
rooms in the house. It is definitely a "period piece,"
with a floor of old pine boards. Between its timbers,
the ceiling is plastered in oyster shell white as are the
walls, while the smoky dark woodwork and fielded
panels suggest countless fires in the hearth, against
all of which the antique waxed and polished furni-

ture glows richly, and wall hung English delft plates
in polychrome sparkle in the light from a tin chandelier.

This, then, is a fittingly dramatic background for
the masses of shining pewter on the beam high Pennsylvania dresser with its scalloped ends and raised
panel doors—the chargers and the row of overlap-
ping trenchers; the six foot line of round bowled
spoons; the shelf of shapely tankards, each one a
work of art; the coffee pots, jugs, and beakers all vie
with the lesser but equally interesting grouping of

64

LIBRARY

Rare oak pieces and fine Whieldon ware grace the fireplace end of the Library where the sheathed chimney breast is ornamented by a fine portrait of Mrs. Chorley.

candlesticks and tureen on the dark, reflective surface of the table top—the board of southern origin at which so many have supped in days long gone by—a ten foot, trestle footed tavern table of pine reinforced with a huge "hutch" that actually forms four capacious drawers. And this is not all.

In one corner of the room is a Pennsylvania cupboard with a glazed upper door, displaying a fine

collection of 19th century American Bell pottery and 18th century English Whieldon ware. On the wall flanking the small rear window is a rare pair of 18th century tinware sconces, so few of which seem to survive, and, at the dresser ends are two Dutch style turned and painted chairs made in New Jersey in the 1800s. These have gay cushions of a red and blue check design which repeats the color and pattern of

65

PARLOR CUPBOARD

A magnificent 18th century sunburst corner cupboard in its original paint is the
glory of the Chorley Parlor, helping display part of the Whieldon collection.

the window hangings. The dining chairs are humble
but impressive Windsors of the early 19th century.

Up a couple of steps and across the Hall is the no
less interesting though far more formal Parlor—a period Salon of great dignity and exquisite taste, extending the depth of the house. Since it has twin
fireplaces it presumably was once two rooms. The
walls and ceiling here also are white, set off with a

deep wooden cornice, and a chair rail and baseboard,
all painted a rich green as are the window bottoms
and the mantelpieces and the heavy doors. In splendid contrast are the opulent window hangings of
scarlet watered silk, suggestive of cardinal's robes,
whose color is repeated in the rare 17th-century
Turkish Oushak rug with its radiant medallion of
beige, blue, and green.

As might be expected, the furnishings here are equally splendid. The recess between the chimney breasts seems made for the tall Salem secretary, bonnet topped and finialed, its tombstone shaped door panels revealing the rich grain of walnut above the slant top desk which forms its base. Its engraved brasses are especially fine, the H-hinges of the cupboard being attached to the sides of the case, while both drawers and doors have delicately worked escutcheons which contrast pleasingly with the bail handles. Further decoration is supplied by the compass design with which the doors are inlaid. According to the experts this bun footed piece was made between 1700 and 1720.

A companion piece to the secretary is an especially fine roundabout chair in faded mahogany, hailing from Philadelphia. In spite of its 1740-50 dating, it is in an excellent state of preservation, intriguing with its serpentine front, and pad feet with tongue carvings. On either side of the secretary are 18th century English chairs of Queen Anne vase-back style, and, close to the right hand fireplace, a 1750 Philadelphia walnut open arm chair, slip seated in black leather.

In one corner of the room is a New York Chippendale wing chair of 1760-1770, in green brocade, and an English birdcage candlestand. At the other end of the room is the most outstanding piece in the collection—a magnificent 18th century sunburst corner cupboard from New Jersey in its original paint. Its exterior a deep red, it has a curved shelf backing in a lighter red. The alternating colors of the sunburst are yellow and green.

This cupboard contains a priceless display of Mr. and Mrs. Chorley's specialty, including a very rare pair of Whieldon crested birds, circa 1755, and a pair of Whieldon 18th century musicians. Two very early pieces are a 17th century standing Lambeth delft salt, and a delft caudle cup dated 1657 in blue and white, the rest of the display being made up of Ralph Wood, Whieldon, and salt-glaze pieces.

Other examples of Ralph Wood ware in green and tan—a shepherd and shepherdess, and a Saint George and the Dragon—make up one of the mantel garnitures. The portrait over these is an 18th century painting by John Wollaston. On the other mantel the garniture consists mainly of Whieldon solid agateware pieces, and the portrait is by an unknown English artist. Worthy of special mention here is a very rare ceramic piece composed of a pair of wading birds in salt-glaze which adorns a fine English gaming table.

Next to the corner cupboard is an 18th century Philadelphia Chippendale lowboy in mahogany. Standing on this are a polychrome bowl and a blue and white "whale" plate, both of English delftware. Over these is a Constitution mirror of 1760 or earlier with a basket finial. Another of the more important furniture pieces is a fine tea table from Newport attributed to Townsend. This stands in front of a Hepplewhite camelback Baltimore sofa of 1785 which has painted floral decoration on the legs, and is upholstered in red watered silk to match the draperies. Above the sofa is a large landscape by James Francis Cropsey painted at the end of the 19th century, and nearby is a Benjamin Randolph, Chippendale style side chair which completes, except for the end and card tables, a most impressive interior.

The Entrance Hall is papered in a striking gray and white reproduction 18th century documentary pattern which gives it tremendous character. The fireplace, doors, trim, and ceiling are off white, the floor being covered by a Feraghan rug with an overall floral pattern on a black background, only the border having a ground of red. On the mantel are three very fine urns in blue john, and a pair of silver and gold modern urns engraved with Japanese scenes. These latter were presented to the Chorleys by Crown Prince Akihito of Japan. Alongside the fireplace is an 18th century firescreen in English needlework which is wholly original, and to the right of this is an English oak lowboy dated 1705, with pointed toe feet. On it is an early polychrome painted delftware bowl.

One of the most striking features of the Hall (in more senses than one) is the handsome tall clock in cherry attributed to Matthew Edgerton of New Jersey, circa 1780. This has a pewter and brass dial engraved by Isaac Brokaw. Against the adjoining wall is a very good 18th century table of cherry made either in Pennsylvania or New Jersey. This has an inserted slate top, a drawer, and delicate legs with pad feet. On it stands a blue and white Bristol delftware bowl on a teak stand, and on the wall above is a Pennsylvania Queen Anne mirror dated between 1720 and 1750, into whose cresting is set a carved and gilt wood representation of the Prince of Wales's feathers. There is also a pair of interesting portraits by Belknap, dated 1826. On the back of one of them the artist has noted the name, age, and weight of the sitter: Jonathan Richards, 47 years, 237 pounds! Under these is a pair of 1750 maple, five-back chairs, both of which have their original rush seats and are

PARLOR

A formal room of dignity and taste, the Parlor has twin fireplaces and a tall Salem secretary of museum quality, chairs, walls of white plaster and twin mantels in oldtime green, resplendent with curtains of scarlet watered silk and a radiant 17th century Oushak rug.

ENTRANCE HALL

The handsome cherry tall clock in the Hall is attributed to Matthew Edgerton.
The slate topped table supports a Bristol delftware bowl below an early 18th
century Pennsylvania Queen Anne mirror. The Portraits are by Belknap.

in perfect condition even to the tiny finials.

Description of the Library is reserved to the last since it is the only room not in period. It nevertheless has a stong feeling of antiquity since all the interior woodwork, including fireplace sheathing and bookcases is made from 150 year old Virginia heart pine, once the flooring of two old Virginia churches that were demolished. The furniture and furnishings are a delightful mixture of antique and modern. One entire wall, separated into two sections by a graceful bow window, serves to display the main collection of ceramics, principally 17th and 18th century delftware. Special pieces of English delft are hung on the wall and over the doorway, and there is a huge 18th century Bristol bowl, 64 inches in circumference and standing nearly ten inches high, on the grand piano.

Among the rare antique pieces in the room is a 17th century Pennsylvania table of oak, ash, and pine, with a cruciform base. Another oak piece of note is an English dressing box dating from 1687.

This is flanked by a pair of simple ladder-back chairs whose provenance may be New Jersey, as is that of a Queen Anne walnut desk dated somewhere between 1720 and 1740. Over the dressing box, and either side of a portrait of the owner, are eight original pencil and watercolor sketches by Thomas Moran (1837-1926) of scenes on Long Island.

Altogether one would label this particular room interior a friendly one, casual but rich in its diversity; a room where one would never be at a loss for a conversation piece—and a fitting modern addition to the rest of the interiors where dignity combines with grace in keeping with the excellence of the antiquities they house.

MEADOWBROOK FARM

The Country Residence of Mr. and Mrs. J. Liddon Pennock, Collectors

DRAWING ROOM

A beautiful cabinet displaying lusterware balances a door to the garden room in
the Pennock Drawing Room. Other pieces are distributed around the room so
that the collection does not dominate the décor.

Lusterware is the particular passion of Mr. and Mrs.
J. Liddon Pennock, and display pieces, both singly
and in groups, have come to be an attractive feature
of several rooms in their modern country residence.
Great pains, however, have been taken to avoid having the displays overpower the décor, or do more
than add a spice of form and color to the whole.
That this aim has been achieved is evident even in
the large and spacious Drawing Room where the

majority of the pieces are confined to one special
cabinet which in itself is a strikingly beautiful piece
of furniture.

Quite incidentally that cabinet balances a doorway which shares one end wall with it, and therefore does not dominate the room as it otherwise
might. The only other pieces displayed in this room
are a pair of Creil polychrome plates on a desk, a
Whieldon shell on the coffee table, and a pair of

DRAWING ROOM

A pair of footed vases over the Drawing Room bookshelves, a Whieldon shell on a coffee table and Creil polychrome plates on a desk constitute accents rather than displays, the colors used matching those of the porcelains so that balance of interest is maintained.

footed vases over the bookshelves—all accents rather than displays.

The part that the porcelains play in the furnishing of the room is therefore consistent with the decorating plan which has produced a unified interior that is entirely pleasing as a whole. Much of this effect is due to the fact that the colors used match rather than contrast with those of the porcelains so that a balance of interest is maintained, and the decorative

value of the display is not overemphasized. On the other hand, since yellow predominates, the net result insofar as the room itself is concerned is an air of light and gaiety on even the dullest of days.

The room colors begin with the sunshine yellow of the draperies tinting the daylight which is reflected by the white carpeting and white ceiling and repeated in the yellows and whites of some upholstery fabrics. The accent colors are green, black, and

DINING ROOM

Light colors and gay paper set off the pink lusterware to perfection, an effect augmented after dark by concealed lighting in the ceiling which also highlights the silverware on the sideboard, the individual pieces such as a porcelain fish, and a Meissen ware duck on the sideboard and dining table respectively.

brown, the furniture pieces in natural walnut, or variously painted yellow, green, or black. The fireplace is of white marble accented by narrow strips of yellow and black, and set off by a hearth rug of rich brown fur.

An architectural effect is supplied by the narrow paper border in dark brown around the cornice, and the deep window pelmets which present a bold leaf pattern in pink, yellow, and white on a gray ground.

Architectural, too, is the ceiling high china cabinet of old pine with its vertical panels and carved cornice molding, its round topped opening bordered with strapwork punctuated with paterae. Originally, this was an 18th century corner cupboard discovered in New Orleans, and made over to stand flat against the wall, with interior lighting to illuminate the shelves. The lower section remains a cupboard with paneled doors.

FOYER

**The sunny foyer gains architectural interest from the wallpaper pilasters and
stair arch. The ceramics are confined to one small cabinet.**

Today the collection displayed on these shelves
includes some Staffordshire ware and some French
Creil, the latter printed in red transfer on the yellow
porcelain. Also of special note is a tea service in
canary yellow Liverpool ware (circa 1800), whose
pattern is in black transfer. This, incidentally, is similar to a set in the Smithsonian Institution museum.

Among the Drawing Room's major furniture
pieces are a loveseat and sofa, upholstered in a yellow stencil print on a white ground; a pair of Louis

XVI fauteuils painted green over white, and upholstered in green silk. In a corner by one of the twin
recessed bookshelves is a late 18th century Carlton
House table in walnut with a gold stamped, red
leather top; in the opposite corner is a chest painted
yellow and green to simulate bamboo. By the fireplace stands a wing chair in olive green and gold,
and in front of the sofa a modern Italian coffee table
finished in *fausse tortue* and bronze beneath its white
marble top.

76

At one end of the sofa is an oval pembroke table in mahogany; at the other a drum table of the same wood; elsewhere a black enameled Chinese-Chippendale chair supplies a spot of color with its yellow velvet cushion. On the walls carved and gilt wood brackets support painted urns, and on the mantel are black metal pastille burners on pediments.

The room's lighting devices vary from a silver candlestick in a hurricane globe to crystal and bronze wall sconces and candelabra, and porcelain based lamps. Those near the fireplace wall are supplemented by concealed lighting consisting of adjustable fixtures in the ceiling. After dark this room looks as gay and inviting as it does by day, and when the porcelains are illuminated by the cabinet lights the display becomes a thing of beauty.

Another place in which part of the porcelain collection is shown to good advantage is in the Dining Room, and this despite the fact that the whole room itself constitutes a panorama of decorative art. Above the dado the walls are covered with a hand painted reproduction of a stunning Chinese wallpaper. On its silver background are painted vines, flowers, foliage, and birds—chrysanthemums and roses in blues, pinks, and reds, leaves of white, pink, and deep blue, birds and flying insects in orange, pink, and brown, with suggestions of nearby landscape and distant hilltops to give the silver sky illimitable depth. With the white ceiling, light gray rug, and white trim, plus white silk draperies with silver borders, the room is permeated with the feel of the open air, which the Adam mantel with its gray and white marble and twin white urns does nothing to dispel. Only the mahogany furniture holds it down to earth, and as a setting for the pink lusterware, the light coloring is perfection.

Artificial lighting is supplied by a central chandelier in an airy modern Italian design with teardrop crystals and tiny prisms, and a delicate frame of gilded brass. In the chandelier's ceiling rose, and at the edges of the ceiling itself are small circular "hidden" lights to provide the basic illumination and spotlight features such as the silverware on the sideboard, the porcelain display in its recess, and individual pieces such as the huge porcelain fish on the serving table and the Meissen ware duck which occupies the center of the dining table between meals.

The sideboard is a late 18th century, spade footed Hepplewhite piece in crotch mahogany, bow fronted and equipped with a brass drapery gallery and decorative pulls of hammered brass. The serving table

FOYER

The end of the Foyer adds an illusion of space by huge mirrors flanking a window wall across which stretches a profuse planting of growing ivy and cymbidium orchids.

also is Hepplewhite, in banded mahogany with inlay; the dining table of the same style and period with a twin tripod base, brass claw feet, and a satinwood inlay border. The chairs are English made reproductions of the Hepplewhite intersecting shield pattern, with plain, tapered legs and dished seats upholstered in brocade of a delicate pink, brass nailed.

Over the sideboard are plain silver twin sconces, and on the serving table are tall glass, twisted stem girandoles, each holding three candles. The great porcelain fish is 17th century French in white and yellow with pink spots; the duck on the dining table an excellent piece of Meissen ware, while the lusterware display represents a good collection of the pink variety, complete with an important tea set in the grape design.

Other examples from the collections are to be

78

DRAWING ROOM

The Drawing Room in its Summer dress with white painted Indian chairs,
tabouret and table in carved and pierced teakwood.

found in the Entrance Hall—a large, sunny Foyer opening off the Vestibule. These, however, have little bearing on the furnishing scheme since they occupy but a part of one small cabinet. The room itself, on the other hand, is quite interesting if only as an example of what can be done with detail.

This room normally gets its full quota of daylight from the great, wall high windows, and some through the wide archway to the Drawing Room which is two steps lower. Across the foot of the large window group is a plant box full of growing ivy and cymbidium orchids, and above it is a hanging basket with a flowering plant. On either side the windows mirror glass extends from the dadoes to the cornices, adding to the illusion of space. The windows themselves are framed with handsome, bead fringed beige draperies hanging from a heavy, black painted metal rod with terminals in repoussé brass. The tie-backs are beige and dark brown, with brown, tasseled cords, and above the center of the window is perched a mounted pair of buffalo horns, which call attention to other similar trophies.

On either side the window bottom is an impressive looking wooden plinth with a decorative panel modeled in low relief. These plinths are bronze colored with black bases, and originally served as pedestals for doorway pilasters in an Italian palazzo. Today they support tall twin candelabra. The walls themselves are of peculiar interest because of the unusually successful adaptation of *trompe l'oeil* decoration they present. They are papered dead white, but on the paper, in dull gold, are representations of Ionic pilasters with plinths, plus dado and cornice moldings. These, naturally, give the whole interior a striking architectural character, all the more effective because the illusion is not at once apparent.

Almost covering the whole floor is a large 18th century Aubusson rug patterned in muted colors (pink, green, etc.) on a background of faded beige. Though the floor center is clear, there are quite a few pieces of notable furniture around its periphery. These include a long, serpentine fronted Hepplewhite table with tapered, reeded legs, and a pair of Hepplewhite side chairs with beige seats similar to those in the Dining Room. On the table are lamps

with alabaster bases, their shades and beaded fringes a light beige, and an alabaster flower urn. On the wall is a Chippendale mirror in carved and gilt gesso, with a gadrooned urn finial spouting grapes. At this same height around the room are a few sculptured animal heads, while modeled birds and other small creatures disport themselves around the flat archway to the Drawing Room.

The rest of the furniture consists of a Louis XVI fauteuil upholstered in pale green velvet; a loveseat in multi-colored striped satin, and a small 18th century painted table serving as a telephone stand. Reserved for the lusterware items is an English Regency cabinet with a cupboard base and vitrine top. This serves to display a collection of cream-glaze pottery with burnished gold trim, most of the pieces being designed to hold matches and therefore providing areas on which to strike them.

Thanks to the variety in the furnishings and the sympathetic but unobtrusive backgrounds provided for the collections, the Pennock residence can be considered an enviable example of enlightened eclecticism in rooms that can never be other than bright and exciting while comfortable and charming —fulfilling the ideal of space and serenity that so many seek and so few achieve.

80

SANS SOU

The Country Residence of George W. Helm, Jr., and George Hickey, III,
Architect and Interior Designer

DRAWING ROOM

The Drawing Room with its great vaulted ceiling, the far wall dominated by a
ten foot Tosa screen, full of lively colors, rich textures and graceful forms.

Once the pool house and gardens of a fabulous Long-Island estate, the residence dubbed "Sans Sou" by its owners (no doubt with tongue in cheek considering its splendid furnishings!) represents an almost unbelievable transformation which Architect George Hickey planned for himself and his associate. The original structure consisted of two tiled dressing rooms flanking a central loggia with a high, barrel vaulted ceiling and a series of arched openings along the sides. From the front, steps lead down to the oval pool, ringed by a limestone verge and set in a grassy lawn. The pool itself is tremendous—larger than the Olympic pools, its owners aver—with formal gardens to one side and a tree rimmed lawn on the other sloping down to a country lane. The walls of the building and its massive square chimneys are of stucco, finished smooth and painted dead white, with roofs of red pantiles.

DRAWING ROOM

High arched windows cast soft light on the furnishings and open up the gardens
and pool to view. At the far end an opening revealing an illuminated display of
blanc-de-Chine Chinese Export animals.

In the remodeling five archways were closed in by
huge french windows, and one was sealed by ma-
sonry to form a recessed panel on the interior side in
which a fireplace was centered. On the entrance
side, a fore-court was added by erecting a thick
wall topped by tiles and pierced by a wide, central
doorway, two short windows and one long one. The
taller window, which opens into a low wing of the
house, is located close to the point at which the wall
turns in a right angle to join a row of garages forming the second side of a large, open court.

The most striking feature of the fore-court wall is
the central double door enframed in the white
stucco. Beautifully carved in dark cypress it reveals,
when opened wide, a spectacular Japanese maple,
and, beside it, a large glazed jardiniere in green and
white from which springs a robust gardenia bush.
Flanking the outside of this doorway are two earthenware tubs crowded with flowers in season. Behind
them, tall, conical yews reach almost to the top of
the wall. Beyond these, along the entire length of
the wall, smaller, tapering evergreens stand out, like

DINING ROOM

The most dramatic feature of the Dining Room is a tall, black and brass Dutch Stove set into a blue and green recess.

soldiers on guard, against the gleaming, dead white background which eventually will become a wall of living green. The unadorned architectural style, the white walls and warm red tiles set in a wide field of beige pebbles, give the fore-court wall and the taller house behind it the appearance of a Mediterranean villa, while tall trees and masses of foliage beyond the roof ridge add to its air of seclusion.

Inside the house itself, the coolness and severity of the exterior give way to the warmth of lively colors, rich textures, and graceful forms, and other evidences of exquisite taste. This delicacy of design undoubtedly reaches its peak in the principal apartment which is done meager justice by the term "Drawing Room." This is a noble chamber, thanks to

the air of spaciousness afforded by the great, round topped windows and the soaring curve of the high ceiling innocent of any interruption by hanging chandelier or distortion by fanciful decoration—all one massive arch that traps the air and light, undivorced from the walls by any change in color.

From one end of the room the scene is dominated by a ten foot long Japanese screen of the Tosa school which hangs above a Chippendale sofa between two doorways, its golden background confined within a black border; its central feature the twisted trunk of a Ginkgo tree with a pyramid of green leaved branches beneath which cavort cranes in black and white with scarlet heads. Looking in the opposite direction, the arching wall centers on a doorway

85

flanked by gold framed paintings—one by Doussout, the other by Walter Stumpfig—but the eye is inevitably drawn toward the opening which reveals an illuminated display of *blanc de Chine* and Chinese Export animals. These stand out against a background of pale sauterne enframed by an 18th century carved Chippendale molding in natural wood tones.

Between these two end walls stretches a sauterne colored rug, bordered in blue and lime, which hides most of the parquet floor. Walls, ceiling, and trim are of an elusive yellowish color called "chamois," and the draperies are of a deep yellow bound in lime. Relieving these are accents of tangerine and Wedgwood blue, with a modern sofa, two Raeburn chairs, and an occasional cushion in tangerine. Two other similar chairs are covered in a medium blue, while a pair of Louis XIII open arm chairs of fruitwood are upholstered in beige and green Fortuny.

Like much of the furniture, the fireplace mantel is 18th century English Chippendale. It has a natural wood finish, with a surround of sienna marble, and its principal ornaments are a pair of Chinese *papier-mâché* figures in bright costumes of red, green, and yellow, with skipping ropes in a flying loop over their heads. Nearby are three unusually fine pieces of furniture, one an 18th century Chippendale melon shaped cellaret in faded mahogany, with reeded and tapered legs, and brass hardware and bindings. This, and another of somewhat lesser importance, act as tables for brass, triple *bouillotte* lamps. The second piece is a remarkable mahogany Chippendale pembroke table of New York State provenance, incorporating such desirable features as a standing cross stretcher which is both pierced and raised, and a top that is molded as well as scalloped, with open scroll brackets. The third is another New York pembroke in mahogany, of Sheraton style with legs that are tapered and reeded, and leaf edges that are double inlaid.

One of the more fascinating pieces, however, is a brass bound French drum with its original vellum head. This is mounted on a special base which the owner had made from a 17th century brass Dutch kettle stand. Other interesting features of the room are an English painted tin tea bin and a coffee bin which are used as end tables. Black enameled, with gold lettering, they make quite different stands on which tall brass lamps and a pair of majolica birds in brown and green are supported.

Compared with the Drawing Room, the Dining Room is small and sparsely furnished but is nevertheless highly decorative thanks to the colors and some ingenious details. Its most dramatic feature is its fireplace—a tall Dutch stove with a decorated castiron base and fuel basket surmounted by a sheet iron flue box, tall and rectangular, projecting several inches from the wall. All of this is dead black, trimmed with polished brass including a picturesque crank and ratchet by which the trammel is raised and lowered. Brass knobs on the front and sides control the dampers. All of this is set into a shallow recess, almost ceiling high, which is painted a deep blue-green to match the wide cornice molding and baseboard. On either side is a small painting—pastoral scenes by Burlinck—in a carved and painted frame.

Balancing the fireplace across the room is an equally unusual feature, a primitive painting, large and square in a flat, black frame. In the picture the blue gray of sky and water predominate, and standing out against this light background a pair of tall, skimpy trees give the whole picture the appearance of a window opening on to a spring landscape. Much of this illusion is due to the color of the wallpaper, an old time reproduction in deep yellow patterned with trailing flowers in deep blue, orange, blue green, and white. The ceiling is a soft yellow, and one wall is covered with shelves displaying books in colorful bindings, and porcelain items, all against a background of deeper yellow. The parquet floor is largely covered by a modern octagonal rug in silvery green, and the two pairs of french windows are flanked by heavy silk draperies in a rich yellow.

Such is the striking and unusual setting which requires no spectacular furniture to give it interest. The dining ensemble consists of an oval Sheraton pedestal table in mahogany with a lipped edge, delightful in its proportions and simplicity and perfect in scale for the room which is scarcely of banqueting dimensions. On it is centered an oval egg bowl of colorful Chinese Export ware in the form of a sitting hen. Around it, against the walls, are half a dozen English Windsor type tavern chairs of yew, with beautiful turnings and pierced splats. For contrast there are two Italian carved Regency side chairs with swan neck finials, providing splashes of color with their mustard yellow upholstered seats.

Several additional Sheraton pieces complete the well scaled furnishings—a small 18th century inlaid mahogany sideboard, with its brown porcelain egg bowl and a pair of yellow shaded *bouillotte* lamps; a

DINING ROOM
Across the Dining Room from the Stove is a primitive painting that seems to open on to a spring landscape like a window.

mahogany side table, its apron and legs inlaid with yew, accompanied by an arm chair. In one corner is a small 17th century round table in oak which has a triangular apron and three turned legs.

The bedrooms in this house are of particular interest largely because of the architectural quality created by exotic wallpaper borders. In one of the lower floor bedrooms, a pair of french doors serves in lieu of windows, opening on to a decorative wrought iron balcony rail. Since a massive four poster bed with tapering, carved and reeded posts and a deep

mahogany tester, takes up much of the floor space, the furniture is somewhat limited. On the other hand, each wall is set off by a wide and vivid paper border in brown, red, green, and tan so that its pale grège surfaces need no other decoration. The draperies are of a plain grège fabric and the carpeting a slightly contrasting sauterne.

A Charleston Chippendale bed, acquired in Boston, is hung with a Fortuny print in strawberry and beige. Opposite the foot is a mahogany Chippendale commode with ogee feet, above which hangs a

BEDROOM

This bedroom wall is set off by a wide and vivid paper border as seen across a Charleston Chippendale bed in a rich Fortuny print. The mirror is Chinese Chippendale.

gilded and pierced Chinese Chippendale fretted looking glass, flanked by a pair of simple brass sconces. On the commode is a pair of Chinese covered vases in blue, green, and gold. In a corner by the french window, a small Chippendale writing table bears a silver inkstand and a candlestick lamp. The chairs are Philadelphia Chippendale.

Even more strikingly architectural than this chamber is the Guest Bedroom whose principal decoration is also a fine paper border, but this one includes garlanded pillars that divide the fireplace wall into panels. This paper border is of a continuous swag design over a flowered ground of gold and green, while the wallpaper itself is a plain robin's egg blue under a ceiling of the same tint. With a high-backed bed on either side of it, the little fireplace is given tremendous importance. The carved mantel with its rounded ends was made from a Venetian valance board, its 17th century gold leaf decoration being preserved. Above this is a tall, gold-framed looking glass with an elaborate cresting that reaches up to the cornice. On the mantel alongside it are marble and ormolu candlesticks, and, centered in the paper panel on either side is an 18th century painting in an oval gilt frame.

Between the fireplace and each bed stands a three stage night table in simulated bamboo, painted a lime green. These match the bed heads whose panels are covered in an orange and yellow cotton print. The bedspreads are of the same material, forming an interesting contrast with the pale sauterne carpeting. The overall effect is one of exquisite detail and simple delight, entirely free of any artifice or obvious contriving—a characteristic of every room within these walls.

CLIFTON

The Plantation Residence of Harry T. Peters, Jr., Collector

ENTRANCE HALL

Nine smiling Chinese figures in porcelain on the mantlepiece greet the new-comer to the Peters residence!

A man of tremendous energy and wide interests, Mr. Harry T. Peters, Jr., is a breeder of Quarter-horses, Shorthorn cattle, Cheviot sheep, and Greyhounds, who still finds time to collect Chinese Export porcelains and Staffordshire animals, old Chinese ivories, fine American 19th century paintings, unusual rugs, and antique English and American furniture—and his house is arranged to make the most of them all.

"Clifton," as the plantation house is called, lies deep in a valley of the Piedmont foothills amid rolling pastures and wooded heights—a perfect setting for the rambling clapboard homestead which dates, in part, from 1750, and today is surrounded by lush gardens and tall boxwood trees that are a perpetual delight.

Two large wings and a conservatory were added to the original house. There is also a large guest house, and the original kitchen—a separate log

PAGODA

This four foot tall Export Porcelain blue and white pagoda stands at the entrance to the Living Room from the Foyer.

LIBRARY

The library shelves provide a striking setting for a collection of Staffordshire greyhounds against the green walls and woodwork.

cabin—now serves as a small guest cottage.

Throughout the main house the various collections are dispersed in interesting, and often associated, groups. Others are used as decorative features in the guest quarters. One of the most striking displays of all is that of the China Trade collection in the Entrance Hall. This is combined with beautiful old Chinese teak furniture (some of the pieces inlaid with cloisonné!); with rare oil portraits of early Chinese merchants, paintings of the clipper ships, and the hongs from which they were loaded with oriental treasures, and a marvelous Chinese rug in blue on beige, all set against a background of sand tinted walls, old chestnut floorboards, and a corner

95

DINING ROOM

A collection of fine American sporting paintings adorns the walls of the
Dining Room, including horse portraits by Edward Troye and Henry Delattre.

fireplace set with blue delft tiles of an unusual pattern.

In this wealth of fascinating objects, however, the real eye-catchers are the amazing porcelain figures on the mantel shelf—nine smiling Chinese figures of the Ch'ien Lung period, dubbed by their owner "The Happiness Boys," and the big, colorful Chinese

Export goose tureen on a marble topped table between two large, green tinted hurricane shades. Also in this room are a three foot tall painted pewter figure of a tea merchant on a pedestal, and an Export porcelain blue and white Chinese pagoda standing four feet high which is almost priceless. These two treasures flank the entrance to the Living Room.

DINING ROOM DETAIL
In one corner of the Dining Room is a cupboard with a collection of Staffordshire pottery, mostly cow creamers, sheep, rabbit and deer figurines.

LIVING ROOM

In the Living Room is a huge case of butternut housing the Mochaware collection—the interior painted white to emphasize the dark coloring of the pieces.

Elsewhere is a very fine early Chinese wall plaque of a falcon which is inlaid with ivory, and attributed to the great artist Ritsuo.

Opening off the Entrance Hall is the Library whose shelves full of rare sporting books provide a striking setting for the collection of Staffordshire greyhounds. These stand out against the greens of walls and woodwork—a color which blends smoothly with the darker green leather of a nail studded wing chair, and the lighter green of a hand made rug from Greece. This rug is a particularly beautiful specimen of needlepoint in a diaper pattern of white and beige, from the collection of Queen Frederika who supplies such designs to local craftsmen. Here also are 19th century English sporting paintings of greyhounds, and some interesting American furniture pieces such as an 18th century Philadelphia roundabout chair, a teakwood coffee

BEDROOM

The porcelain collection overflows into the owner's bedroom with cats on the hearth and birds on the mantelpiece.

table, and a fine Pennsylvania shell-back arm chair.

In the Dining Room are some of the finest American sporting paintings in the owner's collection. Outstanding among them are four horse portraits by Edward Troye (1808-1874), and two by Henry Delattre. Occupying a corner cupboard is a collection of Staffordshire pottery consisting mostly of cow-creamers, sheep, rabbits, and deer figurines. On the triple-pedestal dining table is an almost life size swan of pure white Meissen ware, while the sideboard sports three Chinese Export pieces—a tureen,

and chocolate pots in blue and white. The sideboard itself is also worthy of note, being a Baltimore piece of Hepplewhite design with the bell and husk inlays. A nearby marble topped side table displays a pair of rare English knife boxes of yew wood with Goanese ivory inlay. At either end of the sideboard is a Chinese Chippendale armchair both slip seats being upholstered in pale green striped material. In contrast, the chairs around the table are English Windsors made of yew with pine seats.

The setting of all these treasures—walls, ceiling,

99

GUEST HOUSE

The only collection assigned to the Guest House is a fascinating aggregation of
Chinese carved ivory flowering plants in true colors.

doors, and trim—is a warm buff color, illuminated, as the occasion arises, by a graceful old six branch brass chandelier, and brass candlesticks in hurricane shades on the table and sideboard.

Undoubtedly one of the most colorful rooms apart from its contents is the Living Room, that range of hues being supplied by the sofas and upholstered chairs, all of which are covered in gay chintzes having floral patterns in bright colors. The Portuguese rug, too, has a light buff background, with floral sprays in old rose and blue. The walls and the plas-

terwork of the beamed ceiling are a pale yellow, adding to the feeling of spaciousness and, quite incidentally, helping to counteract the weighty appearance of a huge kas, or cupboard, of butternut with bun feet that houses the Mochaware collection. This piece was probably made on Long Island where it was found. Inside, it is painted white, and, with the doors open, the warm brown and reddish tones of this distinctive pottery, together with its wide variety of shapes, make a brave showing. This cupboard stands between two windows, and in front

101

of each window is a carved Chinese teak pedestal supporting a painted *papier-mâché* figure, one of them representing John Paul Jones "shooting the sun" with his sextant, the other being an English shop figure depicting a gentleman taking snuff. On the mantelpiece a row of handsome graduated bowls in Mochaware forms a colorful garniture. A different style of display is formed by a collection of weather-vanes in this room's bow window.

The porcelain collection overflows into the owner's bedroom where a group of Meissen and Staffordshire swans in a variety of poses and sizes graces the mantel against the tan and green of a lacy documentary wallpaper. An equally large group of Nikko cats quite fittingly occupies the hearth. The crewel work draperies and their pelmets, which have a widely spaced pattern, are of tints harmonizing both with the paper and the crewel work of a pair of wing

GUEST COTTAGE
Even the small Guest Cottage with its horse trophies and pictures maintains the
cozy atmosphere of the main house.

chairs as well as the Greek needlepoint rugs. It is
these muted colors and delicate patterns that constitute the room's greatest charm.

The only collection consigned to the Guest House
is probably the most colorful and delicate of all.
This comprises a fascinating aggregation of Chinese
carved ivory flowering plants in bowls, some of them
mounted on carved teakwood stands. The ivory is
stained to imitate the bright, natural colors of the

leaves and petals which actually seem so lifelike that
one is astonished to find they have no perfume.
These precious works of art are confined to two tall
teak cabinets, or vitrines, with beautiful bronze
hinges and latches, and oddly arranged shelves.
Their tops are graced by a pair of large porcelain
swans.

Ordinarily, few multiple and varied collections
such as are housed at "Clifton" can successfully be

SOLARIUM

Chinese teak and bamboo furniture is well adapted to the light and airy
Solarium or Summer Dining Room adorned and perfumed with tropical plants
and exotic blooms.

intermingled to provide a series of contrasting but
related and equally alluring interiors within a house
that has little overall architectural integrity. That
Mr. Peters has been able to accomplish this is perhaps but a reflection of his similar success in coordi-
nating a wide range of interests in other and more
practical fields, an enviable achievement in itself.

HOPEDENE

The Summer Home of Mr. and Mrs. Charles C. Paterson,
Antiquarians and Connoisseurs

108

DRAWING ROOM

An eye catching feature of the great Drawing Room is this large *cartel* with its attendant group of five porcelains on brackets which dominate one of the central panels. The Louis XIV, XV, and XVI furniture includes several pieces finished in black lacquer, constituting vivid accents among the lighter colored and upholstered pieces thus eliminating any suggestion of monotony.

Though antiquities play an important part in their lives, Mr. and Mrs. Charles C. Paterson do not allow old time furnishings to dominate their surroundings in the mansion they are pleased to call their summer retreat. Both alike consider all-round livability more important than the display of antiquarian treasures, but they also recognize that the creature comfort contributed by overstuffed seating needs the leavening of things of beauty and aesthetic value. All this is evident from the interiors of their Newport residence where modern upholstered pieces have been happily blended with their prized antiques in achieving a graceful and dignified, yet attractive and inviting, series of rooms. So cleverly combined are these sometimes antipodal types of furnishings and bibelots that the contrast is never immediately obvious.

In carrying out this idea of combining beauty

FOYER

This towering white-porcelain stove from Vienna of 1750 dominates the Entrance Hall.

DRAWING ROOM

Subdued colors and patterns form an unobtrusive background to the Formal Drawing Room—furnishings, contributing little in the way of dominating texture or pattern, acting as catalysts rather than as decorative features in themselves.

with utility, it is only natural that the proportions of old to new—and utilitarian to purely decorative—varies considerably from room to room. But one thing to be noted in all these apartments is that the colors are, for the most part, subdued, the walls and rugs and curtains serving as unobtrusive backgrounds to the furnishings, contributing little in the way of dominating texture or pattern, and acting rather as catalysts than decorative features in them-

selves. In the Drawing Room, for instance, where the aesthetic is emphasized and leisurely delight is the keynote, the most striking feature is a wall display of blue and white Chinese porcelains ranging from the Ming through the Kang H'si periods. Perched on their little gilded brackets, each stands out boldly against the pale wall surface, as satellite to the central piece—a large Louis XV *cartel* in black lacquer with ormolu mounts.

111

DINING ROOM

In the Dining Room the background is provided by a wall covering of blue green silk with horizontal shadings and a darker dado, interrupted by striking Louis XVI carvings representing the arts that form the overdoors. Large Louis XV paintings adorn three of the walls, with floor length draperies of off white taffeta at the windows.

Actually, this huge, inviting room is a replica of a former apartment of the Patersons in Paris, and has the same delicate air of distinction without any sacrifice of comfort. Both the ceiling and the heavily molded paneled walls are in off white, and the formal draperies, with their deep, scalloped pelmets, all in cotton damask, are also off white. The unusual rug, with its irregular open pattern—made in Portugal especially for this room—is 17th century Span-

ish in design with blue and yellow on mauve giving way occasionally to flowing areas of yellow ground, all within a narrow yellow fringed border. Thus although the whole design is interesting, it is far from overpowering.

This calculated restraint is evident even in the house itself which is basically Georgian modified by a few late 19th century details. There is a hipped roof set back and balustraded above a huge semi-

circular single story bay, and adorned with a recessed Victorian railed dormer over the main entrance. The walls of alternating dark and light brick, the window trim of light stone with heavy winged keystoned lintels, the lower ones round topped to match the massive stone entrance with its Ionic pilasters and carved and paneled intrados—handsomely striking without being formidable, and complemented by a stone balustraded forecourt, and lawns enlivened by urns and clipped hedges.

Impressively old world is the Entrance Hall of white marble, even to the floor, its carved marble console and seat dwarfed by a towering 12 foot stove of white porcelain from Vienna of 1750—a massive

creation garlanded with roses. Fortunately, this artistic heating plant is built up of 32 pieces (the joints are invisible), so that transportation and assembly problems were reduced. Its firebox is connected to an adjoining room from which it can be supplied with fuel. The Hall actually needs no further ornamentation than this gargantuan creation and work of art upon which the visitor's attention is immediately fixed from the moment of entering, and sets the keynote for the wonders to come, beginning with the Drawing Room itself.

This is one of the largest rooms in the house, supplied with five ceiling high windows. At one end of the room, between two of these windows, is a Louis

SITTING ROOM

Least formal of these rooms yet highly inviting is the semicircular Sitting Room whose triple French windows open on to a pleasant garden and side lawn. A notable feature here is the wall paneling in off white with decorative pilasters and swag draped capitals under an ornamental cornice. On the walls are elegant Louis XVI appliqués in ormolu with Queen Anne mirrors and framed prints alternating, the crimson damask curtains vying in color with the mammoth Kirman rug of beautiful and intricate design.

XV mantel beautifully carved in white striated gray marble. On its shelf is a fascinating 18th century clock with a remarkable case of gilded wood with a tower-like bracket to one side in which the revolving dial is mounted. Other wall decorations, beside the *cartel* and porcelains already mentioned, include several oil paintings of the contemporary Parisian school. The furniture consists of Louis XIV, XV, and XVI pieces, several of them, such as the commode, *bureau-plat,* small writing table, and coffee table, being finished in black lacquer so that they constitute vivid accents among the lighter colored and upholstered pieces, and eliminate any possible suggestion of monotony.

LIBRARY

The Library boasts a carved fireplace wall which is a copy of the Queen's bedroom at Blois, an oak wall cabinet of 1658, and many 17th century English pieces, a room beautiful if gloomy and ideally suited to contemplation.

Each of these black lacquered pieces happens to be of special interest in itself, the commode being a Louis XIV creation with rounded corners and elaborate ormolu mounts and panel inlays, while the *bureau-plat*, which is distinctly Louis XV with its cabriole legs and ornate mounts, plus a deep apron and drawer and a gold embossed leather writing surface, seems to be a forerunner of the notable Carlton House style of English desk. The comparatively modern coffee table has a serpentine apron and cabriole legs, and a decorated top which gives it a distinctly oriental "feel." Other important pieces here include a Louis XVI *canapé* with a gilt frame, covered in striated green velvet, several Louis XV fauteuils in beechwood, an important, though small, armchair signed "Dupain," and an even more interesting—and valuable—bergère from the Palace of Versailles, marked for the apartment of "Mme la Marquise de—" whose name in ink is by now practically undecipherable. This is a beautiful piece, painted and gilded, and upholstered in mauve satin.

Serving on occasion as antechamber to the formal

SMALL DRAWING ROOM OR ANTECHAMBER

Serving on occasion as antechamber to the formal Drawing Room is this Small
Drawing Room which is equally charming in a more intimate manner, its walls
and ceiling a soft yellow, its rug a very fine Louis XVI Aubusson in rust and
blue on a gold ground.

Drawing Room is the Small Drawing Room which is
equally charming in a more intimate fashion. A
square room off the Entrance Hall, also opening into
the large Drawing Room, the Dining Room, and a
glass enclosed semi-circular garden room and tea
terrace, this small Drawing Room makes the most of
the daylight from the terrace with the soft yellow of
its walls and ceiling, and the golden ground of its
great, and very fine Louis XVI Aubusson rug which
is enlivened by touches of rust and blue. The double

doors and wall panels are ornamented with ribbon
tracery executed in plaster, the flat topped entrances
having overdoor panels with floral paintings. The
large gray marble mantel is Louis XV and on it
stands a gilded Louis XVI clock with a golden laurel
wreath around the face. Flanking this are Louis XVI
terra cotta sculptural pieces in glass cases.

On either side of the fireplace is an unusual Louis
XV marquise in beechwood, covered with brown
velvet, with a handsome pair of *Régence* fauteuils

116

BEDROOM

In Mrs. Paterson's bedroom the Directoire mahogany bed is covered with 18th century striped silk in mauve and off white, with side panels of embroidered organdy. The round bed table is an unusual Empire piece in mahogany with a brass gallery; the mantel of white marble supports an Empire mirror.

nearby, upholstered in velvet of a rich, dark blue. A Louis XV commode with a marble top, and a drop front Louis XVI secretary complete the list of major pieces in this comparatively small but thoroughly delightful room which is lighted, after dark, by half a dozen three light, ribbon patterned wall sconces. Special attention, however, needs to be paid to the two very fine paintings flanking the doorway to the Hall. In their original Louis XVI gilt frames, these are exceptional examples of French gouaches of the Louis XV period of military subjects and extremely rare. In the large Dining Room are several unusual decorative features that add much to a room furnished primarily for spacious formality with no attempt to impose an air of undeniable antiquity, though the antique pieces introduced are all of first

117

LOUIS XIV COMMODE
A feature of the Formal Drawing Room is this Louis XIV Commode with its
extravagant ormolu mounts and panel inlays.

118

quality and great artistic and antiquarian value. The background here is a blue green silk wall covering with horizontal shadings that, together with a darker dado, help reduce the vertical effect of the tall windows and doors which, emphasized by the striking and unusual Louis XVI carvings, representing The Arts, that form the overdoors. The result is a pleasantly proportioned, yet stately, room whose formal atmosphere is intensified by the large atmospheric paintings of the Louis XV period which adorn three of the walls, while floor length draperies of off white taffeta with green and white borders add a further pleasant note.

The dining table is a massive mahogany pedestal type set off by a set of extraordinarily handsome ribbon-back Chippendale chairs in mahogany with leather seats. To one side is a Louis XVI painted console with a marble top on which stands a pair of golden Regency wine coolers in vermeil, circa 1804. These are among the finest pieces in the room, vying for attention with a pair of Hester Bateman candellabra and a silver trophy cup on the mahogany, cabriole legged sideboard. The ceramic collections are represented in this room by Worcester tureens, and one of French white porcelain, plus some rare miniature oriental porcelains of the Kang H'si period which form the garniture of the French mantelpiece, and look exceptionally well in contrast with the red and white of the marble.

Least formal of all these rooms is the Sitting Room which, as its name implies, is a place for family gatherings. It is also one of the most inviting, and of more than usual interest because of its semicircular shape, with its wide triple french windows opening on to a pleasant garden and side lawn graced by the statuary pieces mentioned earlier.

The off white wall paneling here is exceptionally fine, having decorative pilasters between the panels with swag draped capitals and stopped flutes, under an ornamental cornice with tiny bracket-like dentils, and paterae. On the walls are elegant Louis XVI *appliqués* in ormolu, with Queen Anne mirrors and framed prints alternating, and curtains of a deep crimson damask to tie the wall sections together.

The rug is a mammoth Kirman whose beautiful and intricate design tells a story. The furniture, on the other hand, is a harmonious mélange of English period pieces—Queen Anne, Chippendale, and Sheraton—with a soupçon of Irish and Dutch. The secretary, for example, is Queen Anne inlaid walnut, and before it stands a carved English chair with eagle finials to the arms—a rarity indeed!

Other outstanding pieces are a pair of Queen Anne walnut cabinets, with glass doors above paneled ones, each holding a matching collection of Worcester, set off by a lining of gold damask. The four side chairs are part of a very fine set having balloon-shaped backs and crowned crestings. These are upholstered in rose red cut-velvet. On either side of the central garden door is an 18th century bachelor's chest in walnut, another window space being occupied by an unusually fine galleried dumb-waiter in mahogany. The Irish piece is a hunt table in mahogany, with drop leaves. Finally, there is a black lacquered 17th century Dutch cabinet which serves to display a Swansea tea service and a coffee service of *porcelaine de Paris*.

One bedroom perhaps will serve to illustrate the level of the second floor décor—that of Mrs. Paterson, who prefers quiet distinction to flamboyance even in this intimate spot. The style is Directoire in a room having a flock patterned paper in mauve under a white ceiling. The Directoire mahogany bed is covered with 18th century striped silk in a mixture of mauve and off white, with side panels of embroidered organdy. The circular bed-table is an unusual Empire piece in mahogany with a brass gallery, marble top, and graceful curved stretchers tied together by an urn turned finial. The mantel is of white marble with carved and reeded pilasters under a huge Empire mirror which is flanked by a pair of bronze medallions. The two most important pieces of furniture in this room—in addition to the bed—are an Empire drop-front secretary desk with ormolu escutcheons and marble top, and a matching commode believed to have been made for the Ministry of Marine on the Place de la Concorde.

LONGUE VUE

The Residence of Mrs. Edgar B. Stern, Collector and Connoisseur

RECEPTION ROOM

Gem-like is the small main floor Reception Room with its delicate colors and pattern of fabrics and furniture, combining hangings in pink with the dark blue and black of the Aubusson and Bessarabian rugs, and the trailing roses of the gay wallpaper.

A pleasant variation of Southern architecture—with a touch of Palladio—characterizes the suburban house designed for Mrs. Edgar B. Stern by the late Charles A. Platt in 1942. Its park-like grounds are covered with pachysandra in place of doubtful grassy lawns, and twin lines of beech trees arch over its long, straight main approach which terminates in a carriage ring around a tall marble fountain. The house itself, flanked by a single story garage block

and a guest house, with their white, stuccoed walls gleaming in the sunshine, is utterly picturesque.

The main entrance to the house is at ground level, with just a suggestion of a projecting pavilion to give it, and the pillared portico above, a feeling of added importance. The doorway is outlined by strong moldings that suggest pilasters and a strongly coved cornice. Above it is the iron rail of the recessed portico whose pedimented roof casts cool shadows over

THE BLUE ROOM

Subdued but striking colors and a mixture of furniture styles are given a touch of formality in the Blue Room by a Queen Anne walnut secretary and dome top corner cabinet, and a French *trictrac* table doubling as a library table. The Chinese rug is in blue and tan, the paneled wood walls painted Williamsburg blue, contrasting with yellow Louis XV chintz draperies.

the central french window with its sidelights and fan-lights, and on the small, six paned windows that flank it. In the tympanum of the pediment above is set a semicircular light. The transverse roof behind the pediment is hipped, with a tall, massive chimney on each end slope. The total effect is one of pure classical dignity, softened by masses of foliage which partly hide the end extensions, suggesting that the main house is larger than it actually is. The lower flanking buildings, with their columns, pediments, and arched recesses enhance this effect.

Inside the house, the gemlike quality of the whole external aspect is repeated in the small main floor Reception Room with its delicate colors, and patterns of fabrics and furniture. Its background is composed of an off white ceiling with a finely molded coved cornice, and an acanthus leaf rosette for the neat ormolu and crystal chandelier; walls

124

papered in a trailing rose pattern on pale gray above a white paneled dado; and a carved Adam mantel in natural wood with a black marble facing and hearth. On the floor are three boldly patterned rugs—two Aubussons and one Bessarabian—sporting colorful floral designs on dark blue or black, with much gold in the borders.

In sharp contrast are the window and french door hangings, floor length in pale pink draped over gilded bows with center wreaths. Other gold accents are contributed by a three part Regency mirror over the mantel which has its original églomisé panels; by tall, gilded sconces flanking it; by table lamps, and by the all over Chinese decoration of an 18th cen-

tury English lacquered corner cabinet. Before the fireplace is a three back, six legged Hepplewhite mahogany settee, upholstered in white, and, facing it, a Hepplewhite sofa with green lacquered legs in the Chinese manner. Between them is a lacquered coffee table with a deep, pierced gallery. By the fireplace wall stands a triple top Sheraton combination gaming and tea table in black lacquer with gold trim, and in one corner is a handsome 18th century lacquered slant top desk with Chinese decoration, and a chair to match. Above this hangs a wall cabinet, finished in the same manner as the desk, behind whose glass door are displayed porcelain pieces against a background of plum colored velvet.

125

DRAWING ROOM

In the Drawing Room the elegance of fine book bindings, colorful fabrics and old mahogany finds place for the owner's unrivalled collection of silhouette portraits by William Henry Brown who specialized in full length figures of famous men of the 19th century.

On the desk top itself are a pair of Chelsea red anchor leaf dishes of considerable antiquarian interest.

Another highly decorative piece is a Chippendale mahogany wing chair with ball and claw feet, covered in maroon material which has a riotous floral pattern in gold, red, white, and green that is definitely oriental. All of these contribute to the room's overall air of light hearted dignity and intimate charm.

On this same floor is the Blue Room which offers a strong contrast with its neighbor both in manner and feel. In the first place the colors are comparatively subdued though striking, while the furnishing is definitely eclectic in its mixture of styles. Here is an Early American rush-seat and a Windsor chair sharing honors with Late Sheraton, and a tall 19th century mahogany whatnot contrasting with a slender, inlaid grandmother clock having bird finials. The principal pieces which add a touch of formality to

this room are: an early 18th century Queen Anne walnut secretary, and a Queen Anne domed top walnut corner cabinet, both with tombstone shaped beveled mirrors; and an 18th century French backgammon (*trictrac*) table which doubles as a library table.

The colors likewise are formal—with the exception of the Chinese rug in blue and tan—the walls being of paneled wood painted the Williamsburg blue to contrast with an off white ceiling and draperies of a yellow Louis XV chintz. At either side the mantel is a twin, three light hurricane sconce, and, above the geometric mantel whose shelf bears a garniture of soft paste vases and plates, is a brass coaching horn.

The two really formal rooms of the Stern residence are the Dining Room and the Drawing Room, and of these the former is the more impressive, largely because of its elegant chinoiserie and the glow of polished mahogany which reflects the sparkle of crystal from chandelier and candelabra. The architectural details of this interior are superb. The cream colored ceiling is adorned with intertwined garlands modeled in the plaster in high relief. From the center of this depends a chandelier of 18th century Irish crystal having an elaborate vase shaped stem and lozenge drops. The plaster cornice and frieze are decorated with Grecian detail which is extremely effective over the 18th century Chinese wallpaper of trees, birds, and flowers. The door and

127

DINING ROOM

Impressive because of its elegant chinoiserie and architectural details, the Dining Room is quite formal, and the pieces of Leeds ware in an open pagoda like cabinet add a touch of interest shared by the pewter trimmed Adam mantel. The room size "Fantazia" rug is a rosy tan with a black design, whose coloring sets off the rich mahogany of the English Chippendale dining chairs resplendent in modern needlepoint.

china cupboard trim, and the opening to a breakfast bay, utilize cove moldings to secure the pagoda effect which is emphasized in the door casing and cupboard by the eared frames and the recessed archways in which they are set.

Between these two features is the fireplace with its pine Adam mantel decorated with pewter swags and medallions, the whole tied together by a pan-

eled dado. The total effect is incredibly rich, and the pieces of Leeds ware in the open cabinet add a further touch of elegance. On the room size "Fantazia" rug, which is of a rosy tan with a black design, stands an 18th century square cornered, twin colonette pedestal style, two part mahogany dining table. This is surrounded by its six mahogany English Chippendale dining chairs resplendent in modern needlepoint. On the table are three candelabra of 18th century Irish crystal.

At the door to the Servery there is a fine 18th century Hepplewhite bow fronted chest, inlaid and banded with satinwood. Over it hangs a late 18th century oval looking glass in a carved and gilt frame, while on its top are several antique bottles in green Bristol glass. Against the opposite wall is a Hepplewhite spade footed sideboard in mahogany, and, by the fireplace a Chippendale mahogany wing chair in a green tone-on-tone fabric.

In the Drawing Room the atmosphere is entirely distinct though equally elegant in a different fashion. The furniture and furnishings are splendid, but this is, unescapably, a much lived in room—a place where family and friends foregather; an interior without pretensions of any sort, homelike, and with an intimate charm of its own. That difference is due largely to the provisions made for comfort; a room benevolently looked down upon by a kindly lady whose portrait hangs over the mantelpiece; to the family portraits scattered around, but equally strongly by the silhouette portraits that cover two wall areas and constitute what is probably an unrivalled collection of the works of William Henry Brown who was active in the field from the 1830s on, and specialized in full length figures. In this collection he portrays some of the most famous men of the 19th century. The displays therefore form a fascinating study that goes far beyond their decorative appeal.

This huge room has a somewhat similar frieze and cornice of Greek design to that of the Dining Room, in the same off white as the ceiling. There are, however, two chandeliers in this room—a pair of rare, 12-light units of Irish glass dating from the 18th century. And the extra light is needed because the walls are covered in a special green woven damask which is not particularly reflective. The mantel is an unpainted Adam piece adorned with 18th century Chinese Export vases which flank the aforementioned portrait. The woodwork here is of hard southern pine, including the paneled dado and decorative door surrounds which have pilaster capitals and projecting cornices. Flanking the fireplaces is a pair of recessed bookcases with separate arched tops, and in the center of each arch is a colorful Chinese Export vase. The shelves below are filled with beautifully bound books, except for one square space in each which is devoted to a trophy. Both upper and lower spaces are illuminated.

One of the room's end walls is almost entirely occupied by a huge 18th century Chippendale mahogany breakfront bookcase with a swan neck pediment and decorative fretwork, the base's door panels being inlaid and banded. Other pieces of importance at this end of the room are an 18th century Hepplewhite serpentine chest of drawers, banded in tulipwood and adorned with three examples of 18th century Chinese Export porcelains; and an English mahogany hunt table whose smooth lines and deep color contrast interestingly with the distinctive patterns and colors of the three Aubusson rugs covering this floor.

The other half of the room accommodates two contrasting Hepplewhite sofas, one with a scrolled back and the other rounded like a French *canapé*, the former in a colorful 18th century needlepoint; the latter in a modest dark green velvet. By the fireplace is an 18th century Chippendale mahogany wing chair, upholstered in a quilted, hand blocked chintz to match the draperies; opposite is an early 18th century Queen Anne walnut wing chair. Strategically placed are half a dozen Adam painted armchairs signed "Joseph Pink." Three of these are grouped around a late 18th century Hepplewhite mahogany card table which is inlaid and banded in satinwood.

Such a room obviously is timeless; the kind of interior that is adaptable to new acquisitions introduced by successive generations. The other rooms also, regardless of their degree of formality and elegance, remain human in scale and, best of all, retain a charm that is enduring because they possess an atmosphere that is both spirited and serene, and can absorb even the bold, colorless accent of a silhouette collection without damage to its basic character.

LE MARAIS

The Island Home of Mrs. Wylie Brown, Collector and Connoisseur

132

FOYER

The architectural character of the octagonal Foyer is emphasized by tinting moldings in two tones of gray. Centered in each wall panel is a crested, vase shaped Venetian mirror in a white ceramic frame patterned in pink and blue. The lantern is an English antique.

"Le Marais," named for the Atlantic salt marshes nearby—the famed Marshes of Glynn immortalized by poet Sidney Lanier—was built in 1957 but its furniture, which is mostly English and some French, had been acquired over a period of forty years, each piece being selected for some specific location in the home of that period. Due notice was taken of this in designing the present house. The result is a residence whose interiors have been planned to provide the atmosphere of a pleasant and comfortable home, incorporating certain furniture treasures and decorative features while avoiding any suggestion of mere display.

In planning this latest of her homes, Mrs. Wylie Brown had the advantage of knowing exactly what pieces each room should contain, the amount of space required, and the style of décor that would be called for. The result is a totally delightful set of

DRAWING ROOM

Many windows and light colors—yellow, chartreuse, and celadon—add to the cheerfulness of the formal Drawing Room whose furniture once graced the owner's Paris apartment. The finest piece is an inlaid Sheraton 18th century bookcase-secretary, in which are displayed a variety of porcelains and Chelsea figurines.

interiors in the English manner with French detail, all well suited to the semi-tropical climate, and in which her collections of china, silverware, and paintings form an unobtrusive part of the decorative backgrounds.

The house is a charming interpretation of the French *maison de campagne,* of stuccoed stone with a black slate roof. The stucco is tinted gray, but the quoins, window bottoms, wood trim, shutters, and brick chimneys are all painted white, constituting a happy contrast that adds much to the already attractive exterior. All the principal rooms are large, with high ceilings and wide, floor length windows, those overlooking the gardens being of the french type, so that the rooms are exceptionally light and airy. All walls, except those of the Entrance Hall, have uninterrupted plaster surfaces from cornice to baseboard, giving Mrs. Brown a free hand in planning decorative detail. The results are amazing, not only in point of the distribution of masses, but also as

DRAWING ROOM

regards the surface tones which reveal an exceptional color sense, and the differences in mood that can result from the knowledgeable use of even the most delicate tints.

This expert choice of color and pattern is obvious also in the upholstery materials and hangings. Furthermore, the obvious rapport between architect and client in tying together the interior architectural details—the surface textures, the proportions, molding designs, trim, mantels, sash, doors, and so on—is little short of astonishing. This unity of purpose is very well exemplified by the Entrance Hall, or

Foyer, which shows color, form, and interest without the slightest straining for effect.

The entrance door opens into this octagonal space whose four principal walls, innocent of doors or passage openings, have molded panels. While the ceiling and walls are off white, these moldings and the trim are tinted two tones of gray, emphasizing the three-dimensional effect and thereby transforming the commonplace into the dramatic. On the floor is black rubber tile with a scattering of square white inserts to break the monotony and form an attractive pattern. This flooring extends out into one of the two

135

DINING ROOM

The Dining Room furniture includes four original Hepplewhite armchairs. The side chairs and table were made from an extremely old guild table early in this century. In the Chippendale secretary is displayed part of the owner's 18th century English silverware collection, other pieces being set out for use on a Sheraton sideboard and matching console tables.

branch hallways and across the foot of the staircase.

From the center of the Foyer ceiling hangs a highly decorative brass framed hexagonal lantern of English design with scrolled ornament, and holding three candles. This is an antique piece of which a duplicate was made in order to light the hallway leading to the bedrooms, since both of them are visible at the same time. This Foyer forms a perfect setting for a few well placed furniture pieces. Centered in each of the four large wall panels is a

crested, vase shaped Venetian mirror, engraved with a central figure, and set in a white ceramic frame which has a floral pattern in pink and blue. Below them are a pair of Sheraton painted satinwood chairs with seats in green silk, and two English, three drawer stands, the latter adorned with colorful Worcester vases filled with flowers and foliage according to the season.

In one of the long halls opening from the Foyer is a very fine English, three leaf, inlaid card table,

while at the far end is a handsome marquetry chest over which hangs a gilded, carved wood and gesso Adam mirror with floriated rococo scrolls. In a corner nearby stands a dainty "grandmother" clock, while beneath an adjacent window a splash of positive color is supplied by a mass of flowers in a huge black Wedgwood jardiniere.

Off this hall is the Library whose walls are a rich blue green, with the ceiling and trim in off white. The rug is a geometrically patterned Bokhara in deep tones of red with touches of blue. Against these backgrounds the chinoiserie chintz of the sofa with its pattern of blues and grays stands out strongly. A pair of early Empire open arm chairs in celadon bro-

cade; a mahogany wheel-back chair with a white fabric slip seat, and a bergère in crimson brocade, all supply lively accents that contrast with the inlaid mahogany writing desk, the paintings in carved frames of bright gold, and the several pieces of blue and white delft on various occasional tables, all of which add to the air of informal cosiness.

Off the other hall is the Dining Room which, as might be expected, is much more formal. The background colors here are all charmingly delicate, including the carpeting which is of an exquisite celadon tint. The window hangings and their long, sculptural pelmet are of a Fortuny print in an almost matching gray green pattern against a white

LIBRARY

The Library walls are blue green, the ceiling and trim off-white, the rug a Bokhara in reds and blues, the chinoiserie chintz of the sofa patterned in blues and grays, the upholstery of the chairs supplying touches of celadon, white, and crimson.

ground. The room walls are off white, with the ceiling and trim a shade darker. In this effulgent setting the mahogany and maroon leather of the furniture gain an added richness. The four armchairs are original Hepplewhite with intersecting loop backs and triple feathers, the tapering legs turned and acanthus carved—an extremely handsome design with brass nailed seats upholstered in red leather. The eight side chairs and the triple pedestal Sheraton table were made forty years ago from the wood of an extremely old and massive guild table.

In a tall, flat topped mahogany Chippendale secretary are displayed some pieces from Mrs. Brown's 18th century English silverware collection, against a background of antique rose red Italian damask. Elsewhere there is an inlaid Sheraton sideboard, together with a pair of matching console tables on which other antique silverware pieces are set out for use, or decoration. These include a wine cooler, trays, and George III candelabra of T. Barker's design, as well as a delicately chased tea service of Victorian vintage by George Fox. On the dining table itself an 18th century Waterford vase holds masses of garden fresh blooms.

The largest and airiest of these apartments is the Drawing Room which has several french windows and a large bay that flood it with sunlight or lend the light a sunny tinge on gray days by filtering it through draperies of a pale yellow silk. The walls are tinted a delicate chartreuse, while the carpeting is of the same celadon hue as that of the adjoining Dining Room. The ceiling and trim are off white, and the slip covers a pale yellow with floral patterns in black and white.

The furniture in this room is a pleasing mixture of French and English pieces which formerly graced the owner's apartment in Paris. Of these pieces, undoubtedly the finest is the inlaid Sheraton mahogany bookcase-secretary dating from the 18th century. Besides books in fine bindings, this contains a variety of porcelains and Chelsea figurines. In front of it stands an English wheel-back chair in mahogany with a drop-in seat, and on the wall are crystal and ormolu sconces in a wheel motif design.

Across the room is the fine Adam mantel in the same off white as the trim, with a fillet of black marble around the fire opening. On the mantel shelf are disposed Chelsea figurines and candlesticks, with a painting in a bright gold carved frame centered over them. In one corner, by a french window, is a handsome four drawer, serpentine fronted inlaid commode in faded mahogany with a marble top. On

it stands a French shelf clock dated around 1700. A similar type of clock is located on an octagonal card table by the secretary.

Huge English Chippendale bookcases in carved mahogany flank the doorway to the entrance hall, and a variety of small tables mark the conversation groupings. The most unusual of these is undoubtedly a tall, triangular one of walnut which has three cabriole legs and a molded gallery around the sweeping curves of the top. Less of an oddity and more appealing is the curule legged coffee table with an inlaid top which serves a sofa near the fireplace. In the bay window is another sofa, this one a Georgian-style serpentine-backed piece with an elaborately carved mahogany frame and upholstered in green damask. Fronting it is a low spider-legged table of exceptionally graceful proportions. In place of lamp tables there is a marble topped small chest either side the fireplace. These are of English burl walnut with carved and gilded mounts.

This variety in tables is reflected in the seated pieces which range from Louis XVI to late Sheraton; from 18th century English to late Empire, not overlooking the modern upholstered units. And, strangely enough, though so far from the stereotyped, the room loses nothing of grace or dignity while gaining in comfort, thanks largely to the background colors and textures and architectural integrity, an ideal that so many fail to achieve and more are afraid to attempt.

STOKE POGES

The Country Residence of Mrs. John Wintersteen, Collector and Connoisseur

142

DRAWING ROOM

The beautiful parquet flooring forms a perfect background for the Chinese ceramic pieces and the beige brocade slipcovers, while the peach colored walls perform the same service for the varying styles of paintings. Under the balcony is the great carved and gilt marble-topped table of rococo ram's head design.

Despite poetic connotations, "Stoke Poges" has little in common with a churchyard, and there is nothing elegiac about it. Nevertheless it has a great deal to do with Art, its owner, Mrs. John Wintersteen, being a noted connoisseur, President of The Philadelphia Museum of Art, and a collector of paintings whose home gives shelter to many famous canvases when they are not taking part in loan exhibitions.

The Wintersteen residence originally was a stone farmhouse built in 1780. A new wing was added in 1830, and a second one much later. The latter contains a very large room which is practically an art gallery in itself, except for the fact that, thanks to skillful furniture arrangement, it still remains a comfortable, yet elegant, Drawing Room in which pictures are the principal decoration. These pictures, however, do not monopolize the attention or minimize the home atmosphere. On the other hand, al-

SITTING ROOM

The little Sitting Room in its pictures and ceramics is devoted principally to
dogs, with two canvases by Sir Edwin Landseer showing a variety of breeds. The
interior is white, the furniture and carpet in rich reds.

most every picture is clearly visible from any part of
the room, a fact which is likely to impress anyone
entering the room from the main floor of the house
which is several feet higher. Here the two doors,
from the front and rear passageways respectively,
open on to a railed balcony or platform extending
across the width of the room so that it is necessary to
descend several steps to the room floor.

At the far end of the Drawing Room are two windows, with two more in the right hand wall. At the
middle of the inner wall, is a projecting chimney
breast centered upon a delicately handsome Adam
mantel. In this way the interior walls are divided
into a series of spaces of varying widths and heights
(the latter due to tall furniture, mantel, and balcony) in which pictures can conveniently be hung.
The walls are peach colored, and the draperies of
two toned watered silk in related hues. These contrast delicately with the off white of the trim and
molding. In this setting, the oak parquet floor is a
perfect foil for the beige brocade of three sofas—one
between the end windows, two flanking the fireplace

144

The varied yellows of walls, rug, and draperies invest the Dining Room with a sunny glow showing both Chippendale furniture and the pictures to their best advantage.

at right angles. The fireplace itself presents the pale, antique tan of unpainted wood, and the mantel surround adds a further touch of pink patterned with white veining. An occasional soupçon of rose pink is contributed by the upholstery of half a dozen Hepplewhite and Chippendale chairs.

Among the other more important pieces of furniture is a massive Georgian English carved and gilt marble topped table of rococo ram's head design; a carved Chinese pattern table in teak; an ormolu mounted lamp table with a glass top over Wedgwood inserts; a low table in red and gold Chinese lacquer; a black lacquered armchair upholstered in a black, gold, and red tapestry of medieval design, and a mahogany Hepplewhite style card table.

The most colorful items, however, are a pair of three-foot-tall blackamoors in Venetian costumes of red, gold, and yellow. These constitute the bases of candlesticks placed so as to cast light on Degas's painting: "La famille Mante," which hangs on the wall. Close runners-up are half a dozen Chinese pottery, drum type garden seats which serve admirably

145

MASTER BEDROOM

The basic color of the Master Bedroom is blue contrasting with the bed hangings of two toned silver damask over a multi-colored chintz on beige. Between two windows is an heirloom Sheraton secretary-bookcase with an ivory bust as finial.

as sofa end tables. These are in both hexagonal and round shapes, with famille-rose decoration in greens and pink on a white ground. Almost equally exotic are a pair of ebony sconces with ormolu mounts on the balcony wall. Nearby, under a powerful Matisse painting: "A Woman in Blue," (1937), is an English gilt shelf clock by Graham. Some of the table lamps have tall Japanese porcelain vases as bases; others use a richly decorated Japanese vase or a pottery figurine.

The art works are, of course, the most important feature of this room, if not its *raison d'etre*. Beside the Matisse and Degas pictures already mentioned there is another Degas canvas, "The Singers," a large

146

study in charcoal on pink paper by Toulouse-Lautrec, and a small Renoir nude in a heavy baroque gilt frame, and a Rouault. But the most fascinating feature of the display is a group of six paintings and four drawings by Picasso which illustrate his development and changes in technique over the years. The earliest of his paintings in this collection are: "Le Bouquet," (1901); "Boy with a Bouquet" (1905); "Tête de femme" (1908); a small 1922, classic-period painting; and "The Bird Cage" (1942). The rest are unlabeled, the most recent work being a large impressionist canvas—hung over the sofa between the end windows—which was painted in 1961.

Other pictures by important artists are distributed throughout the house, including a scene by the French impressionist, Vouillard, mounted over the carved mantel in the Foyer. In this large, square room, the fireplace is English, and there are a number of interesting and worthwhile pieces of sculpture, paintings and other objets d'art, including blue and white porcelains which the owner has acquired in her travels in such far off places as Japan, Egypt and Thailand, as well as nearby Mexico. There is also a very large, and quite enchanting oil by Franklin Watkins of one of the owner's pet poodles, "Lucky."

The most impressive piece of furniture here is a tall French Renaissance cabinet of carved oak inlaid with marble, which has an air of great antiquity. The rest of the pieces are early American and English, except for a brass knobbed, red velvet cushioned iron seat probably originating in Spain.

Down a few steps from the Foyer is the Sitting Room which seems devoted principally to dogs, and Sir Edwin Landseer holds his own with two canvases of groups of various breeds. His is the place of honor over the mantelpiece which he shares with several Staffordshire-ware dogs. A similar piece forms the base of a lamp by a fireside seat. The other dog paintings, which are quite old—and quite good—are by unknown artists.

This room, with its white interior and beamed ceiling, plain, recessed fireplace, and batten type cupboard door with strap hinges, seems suited to the kennel theme, but its floor and furniture pieces are endowed with a ruggedly rich, and masculine, air by the deep reds and bold patterns of the plaid rug and the upholstery of an easy chair, a loveseat, and an overstuffed sofa. The sofa table is an oversize butler's tray; the end tables a drum type in bright brass

to match the fireplace accessories. By the single window is a very fine slant top mahogany desk.

In the Dining Room there are but three canvases, one a landscape by Derain; one a 19th century portrait by Walter Stuempfig of the youngest son of the family with his two dogs climbing an iron spiral stair; the third a delightful portrait of La Duchesse de Berri in a gorgeous Scotch plaid hat with plumes, done by Sir Thomas Lawrence (1769-1830). This latter hangs in a rococo gilt frame bearing the royal initials over a marble topped serving table of Chippendale design, in company with silver candlesticks and wine coolers, and a porcelain tureen, yellow banded on white with a gold knob and handles.

The "stair" picture, across the room, is also gold framed, and beneath it is a large, galleried Chippendale tea table in mahogany. On this stands an exquisite silver tea service, the repoussé kettle resting on an equally ornate spirit lamp stand. The third painting, with its silhouetted trees, is paired with a serpentine fronted Irish mahogany sideboard whose garniture consists of a silver urn and a pair of entrée dishes.

At the far end of this room, double doors opening into a tile-floored informal dining porch are spanned by an oval fanlight. Beyond are tall windows overlooking the garden—a perfect setting for Brancusi's famous brass, Mademoiselle Pogany. On either side the inner doorway is an 18th century mahogany pedestal upon which stands an urn shaped knife box. In the center of the floor is a twin pedestal Chippendale mahogany dining table surrounded by its 18th century chairs which have black leather seats. Underlying all is a magnificent French needlework rug patterned in black on a pale yellow ground.

The yellow of the rug; the lemon color of the heavy, floor length, white fringed hangings, contrast but mildly with the warm yellow of the walls which is relieved by the white trim. Together they invest the room with a sunny glow regardless of the light, and show the paintings to their best advantage.

In the Master Bedroom, as in others, the tone of the furnishing is augmented by the presence of pictures—mostly small—by important painters. In this room the basic color is blue, the walls being covered with horizontally striated pale blue fabric. The trim also is painted a pale blue, and the watered-silk draperies are of a slightly darker tone than the walls, while the floor carpeting is a gray blue. A pleasing contrast is afforded by the hangings of the mahogany Chinese-Chippendale bed whose reeded posts almost reach the ceiling. These hangings are of two toned silver woven damask over a multi-colored chintz with a beige background.

Here there is also a handsome 18th century wing chair which follows closely as to color with a silvery toned velvet, but the Hepplewhite bench at the foot of the bed is upholstered in a beige woven damask. A bold accent is provided by a carved and gilt Chippendale mirror over a mahogany dressing table, and, between two of the windows, interest is focused on a tall, 18th century Sheraton inlaid walnut secretary-bookcase—an heirloom—which has a pierced scroll pediment with a small ivory bust as finial.

Even in these surroundings the watercolor by Andrew Wyeth which hangs in a corner immediately catches the eye—water, boat, figures, wharf, shadows and evening sky! Below it, in wry contrast is a child holding a cat—a fragment, but by Foujita! Elsewhere there are several Picasso etchings and a lovely watercolor of pink flowers by Demuth. Finally, over a tall chest, in the shadows of two porcelain figurines—one Japanese Kakiemon and one early Imari—is a 17th century painting of a child, the work of Benjamin West (1738-1820), all a fundamental part of a charming country house where Art is king!

THE SEASHORE RESIDENCE OF

George H. Clark, Antiquarian and Interior Designer

152

DINING ROOM

The Dining Room walls are covered with a French chintz in old red, cold
yellow, blues and greens on a light putty ground copied from a bedroom in
Fontainebleau; the furniture is natural polished woods.

The main portion of George H. Clark's summer retreat was built in the late 18th century, and in the
course of time changes and additions were made in
the Cape Cod manner. The final remodeling into a
delightful seashore residence was performed by Mr.
Clark in order that it should not only afford the required accommodation but better lend itself to the
series of exquisite interiors he had planned.

Rehabilitation of the garden was carried out at

the same time to provide the house with a setting
more in keeping with its new dignity. Shaggy pine
trees were removed, lawns and flowering borders
laid out, shrubbery planted, and, best of all, a tall
privet hedge of considerable age and vigor was
transplanted to the site. Square trimmed and cut to
varying heights joined by sweeping vertical curves,
it not only provides a maximum of privacy but adds
a distinctive architectural quality to the garden

LIVING ROOM

The character of the Living Room owes much to the chevron band rug designed by the owner in Ming yellow and light putty. The walls duplicate the yellow of the rug. A feature of the room is the wall sized bow window providing a view over the garden.

which is emphasized by statuary pieces placed at strategic points throughout the grounds. The house itself has siding of cedar shakes, while the trim is painted a warm reddish-brown, a combination which adds distinction to old-time simplicity. Thin pilasters painted a brown black, plus a pair of eight foot decorative ivy trees flank the entrance door to give it weight and importance.

Inside the house, a feeling of spaciousness is achieved in a tiny Foyer by means of a fine French documentary paper patterned in cornflower blue and orange on a green blue ground. The floor is delicately spattered in fine white spots on a *tête-de-negre* ground, in common with all other floors in the house. The wood trim is colored avocado green, in delicate contrast to the darker green of the woolen stair carpet, the whole constituting a perfect setting for the single piece of furniture—a splendid English Regency pine bookcase with brass details. On this are several pieces of Italian soft paste porcelain, an

154

Italian tôle coffee pot, and a *bouillotte* lamp.

Two small rooms in the original section of the house now form a spacious and inviting Living Room which has three exposures, one of them a dramatic floor to ceiling, small paned bow window overlooking the garden. Contributing to the light and airy feel of this room is an unusual rug, designed by the owner, in alternating chevron bands, one colored Ming yellow, the other a light putty, plus a six inch knotted wool fringe in the same tones. The ceiling is oyster-white, and the walls duplicate the yellow of the rug, affording an excellent setting for the many furniture pieces in natural wood, most of them European antiques.

The original pine mantel, stripped to its natural wood tones, is unusually well scaled. Over it hangs a French genre painting of the Louis XV period, and the French tôle figurines on the mantelpiece might well have stepped out of that country scene. Here also is a singular pair of Lombardy poplars carved out of wood, enchanting in form and *trompe l'oeil* coloring. These and the rest of the mantel garniture were probably 18th century toys. On either side the great bow window are architectural cabinets displaying a dessert service in English Liverpool ware in green and raisin brown on a pale sand body.

The furnishings of this room run the full gamut of French and Italian 17th and 18th century furniture, with a small amount of English ornament. In the bow window is an oval 17th century Italian table

155

MASTER BEDROOM

In this Master Bedroom the whole ceiling is tinted pale blue, and the walls are covered with Italian cotton damask in avocado green with galloon edging. Night tables are contrived from hayracks in iron.

in very dark walnut, plus an Italian 18th century open arm chair, and a beautiful Louis XVI small bergère in old brown leather. At the opposite end of the room is a Louis XV country sofa covered in quilted *tête de nègre* linen, highlighted by needlepoint cushions designed from old French playing cards. The cushions are two of a complete set used in this room. There is also a Louis XVI Italian commode, with an Italian gilt mirror, which holds a large black coromandel planter, all of which add a vibrant mass of color to these cold yellow walls.

The small tables of this room vary from an Italian church bench and a Louis XIII stool to an Italian lady's slide top desk. There is, in addition, a large pair of modern chairs in off white French cotton damask, and other small chairs upholstered in sour green and wood brown. Not to be overlooked is an interesting pair of Italian crèche figures, about six inches tall, whose faces are done in wax. These fittingly round out an interior that is full of pleasant surprises without being in the least flamboyant.

The same color scheme as the foregoing is adopted for the small Dining Room, except for the

156

MASTER BEDROOM
An outstanding feature of the Master Bedroom is a five piece toilet service in
Régence red lacquer decorated in gold, including an easel looking glass.

walls which are covered with a superlatively repro-
duced French chintz in old red, cold yellow, blues
and greens on a light putty ground, and finished
with a yellow galloon. This chintz is a copy of a
brocade designed by Philippe de la Salle (1723-
1805) for one of the bedrooms in Fontainebleau
when redecorated for the court of Louis XVI. This
wall covering forms an exciting background for the
furniture in natural polished wood. These pieces
consist of a French Louis XVI round country table
in fruitwood, and two pairs of French Régence
chairs, the fauteuils having leather arm and seat

pads in a faded red, while the cane chairs are su-
perbly carved, with unusually interesting stretchers.

In one wall of this room, tall French windows
open out on to the garden. In the opposite wall, two
small windows are enhanced by pairs of short fes-
toons and cascades in carved and gilded wood, perfect in scale for the room and making further window adornment unnecessary.

Over the dining table is suspended a small French
chandelier of crystal and tin, and another beautiful
ornament is a very fine gilded wood 18th century
barometer whose elaborate decoration terminates in

157

GUEST ROOM

Three alcoves are formed in the Guest Room by cupboards built into the corners, one of them harboring a daybed, another a bed, and a third a Louis XIII walnut desk. The bed is a Lombardy tester type covered in geranium red linen.

a cresting composed of a pair of lovebirds. A large tôle tray and tôle lamp decorate an Italian fruitwood commode, and, under all, is a handmade textured rug in saffron yellow.

One of the surprises of this house is a tiny second stairway which rises from the Dining Room, with walls finished in a soft bittersweet tone. Upstairs, the decoration of the bedrooms is equally well

planned, achieving individuality while making the most of a limited space and sloped ceilings. In the Master Bedroom the ceiling, including a sloped section, is tinted a pale blue, while the walls are covered with a specially dyed Italian cotton damask with galloon edging, both of them in avocado green. The curtains, hanging from polished brass poles, are of natural linen with a narrow green tuck. Under

these are Roman shades in multicolor stripes which add a dramatic touch.

There are a number of especially interesting accessories in this room, the rarest—and richest—being a gentleman's five piece toilet service in Régence red lacquer decorated in gold. This set consists of an easel looking glass, two large boxes with hinged lids, and a smaller box with a pin-cushion top. On either side the bed are console night tables ingeniously contrived from Italian stable hayracks in iron, painted black and fitted with semicircular wooden tops. These support a pair of colorful *papier mâché* figures, and a pair of bronze based lamps. Between these tables extends the headboard which

is made from a beautifully carved antique French panel in its original, warm, natural tone. The bedspread is the same cotton damask as the avocado wall covering, and contrasts well with the vibrant orange upholstery of a chaise longue and a tufted chair. The only other pieces are a Queen Anne side table (unusual in having a stretcher), and a George I dresser. Over the latter hang a number of Régence wood carvings, flat and rectangular, with accents in gold, and a drawing by Charles LeBrun (1619-90).

On this same floor is a large Guest Room which is of particular interest because of its architectural treatment designed to make the most, visually, of the available space. Two alcoves were formed, one

160

by building cupboards either side the window, the other by installing similar storage units in the corners under a roof slope. A third alcove already existed under a dormer window. The total result is a room with a cross shaped floor plan in which the cupboards are barely noticeable, being covered with the same self striped natural Belgian linen as the walls. The window and bed curtains and pelmets are of the same material, the latter set off with inch wide bands of green galloon.

In two of the alcoves are a bed and a daybed at right angles to one another. In the third is a large and impressive Louis XIII walnut desk with iron hardware. The fourth space is occupied by the room door and a French dresser. The bed is a Lombardy tester type, its flat top frame covered with linen which also forms the outer surface of the bed hangings. All the hangings are lined with an intense India print of strong sour greens and geranium reds. The spread is of a flat Duponi silk in geranium red with a wide, contrasting band in the same raw linen color as the walls.

In the dormer alcove is set an Italian daybed, dressed in the same manner but with more of the striking India print visible since a small area at the bed end is covered in this material. At either side of the tester bed are tables cut down from a large 17th century Italian table. On these are tall pewter candlesticks with fabric shades, one having an English Staffordshire figurine in addition.

A problem chamber was the small Guest Room whose treatment, though simple, is astonishingly effective. The walls and ceiling are paneled, and these, along with the floor and trim are painted a dark putty color that ties everything together. In this uniform setting is an excellent example of an Italian Directoire daybed in fruitwood, covered with a green Duponi silk—a fabric not commonly used in this country. Much of the wall area over the bed is given both color and interest by a series of large and colorful military prints and French trade prints, framed in gold so that they stand out sharply against the dark paint. Along with them is a pair of wood and iron candle sconces of French origin.

Equally effective against this dark background are the pale blue of the carpet, and the window hangings of chintz in green and brown with touches of yellow and white which, with the pictures, provide the desirable gay relief called for in a limited space where busy pattern and vivid accents would be undesirable.

Altogether this seems a very satisfying house, from both practical and aesthetic standpoints, in which to live and entertain.

CONVERTED MILL

The Residence of R. Hatfield Ellsworth, Antiquarian and Specialist in Oriental Art

SUMMER LIVING ROOM

A collection of Toby jugs is a feature of the Summer Living Room whose
window wall overlooks the water. The furniture is informal Early American
with a rare Queen Anne armchair in cherry, an unusual Tracy Windsor and a
Rhode Island banister-back chair painted blue.

For almost 250 years the foundations of the present
country home of R. Hatfield Ellsworth supported,
first, a sawmill, then a gristmill, powered by a rock-
bound stream that runs through his garden, suitably
dammed to form a picturesque lake and waterfall.
Today those same foundations uphold the walls of a
residence of antique flavor, retaining the sound por-
tions of the old mill frame, with additions constructed from the fabric of three ancient houses that
were doomed to be demolished.

The old sluice is now in process of becoming a
deep, rocklined swimming pool beneath the same
roof. This occupies a lower floor which can be
opened to the outdoors by massive sliding portals,
and is probably unique. The exterior of the building
is covered with thick vertical pine siding which
turns silvery with age and contrasts interestingly
with the faded orange of the doors and the olive

DINING ROOM

American, Dutch, Chinese, English and Scottish items are combined in the unusual Dining Room built around a mid-17th century walnut dining table ten feet long. The maize colored rug was loomed in India for this room while the chairs are Charles II period japanned black, with olive green cushions.

green window trim. The result is a building that is fascinating in appearance, set in natural surroundings of gray rock, rushing water, widespread elms and crowning foliage so spectacularly beautiful as to be almost beyond credibility.

Surprisingly enough these exotic surroundings have much in common with the man made beauty of the treasures within the house, where exquisite Chinese furniture shares space with European art and things of early American craftsmanship. Some inkling of what is to be expected is revealed by the

square entrance hall whose most conspicuous feature is a Georgian book stand with candle brackets, holding a 17th-century illustrated edition of Gerard's *Herball*, opened at one of its most decorative pages.

To the right of this Hall is a small room with a paneled fireplace wall. This is the Library which is not much larger than the Hall itself. As in other instances, the size of the old paneling determined at least one dimension of the room. The floor, too, is an old one of pine colored with its original red pigment. This tint goes very well with the light mustard of the

168

DINING ROOM

Also in the Dining Room an English bridal chest of yew bearing three family crests supports a Ming bowl, dated 1605, over which hangs a Japanese two panel screen depicting foreign dogs of the whippet type in polychrome on gold leaf.

walls, dado, trim, and muntins and the shelf edging of a built-in bookcase which occupies one wall alongside the door. The ceiling is oyster white. The curtains of linen and wool damask and their matching pelmets are the color of the walls, while the rug is a late 18th century Kashan in a pattern of blues and reds that almost obliterate its golden ground. This rug is particularly interesting since it is made of

silk and seems to change color with variations in the light.

Against this backdrop, the mixture of American and English furniture, spiced with a touch of the oriental and exotic color accents, has an unusual feeling of integrity which adds to its charm and air of cosiness. There is a nice 18th century Chippendale sofa covered with a Williamsburg reproduction

ORIENTAL ROOM

The Oriental Room is reserved for the Ellsworth collection of early Chinese furniture favored by intellectuals of the Ming ruling class and contains 16th century armchairs, 17th century camphorwood chests, a couch and garden seats in rosewood and smaller objects including the 1700 year old stone bear once the leg of a sacrificial altar.

of green and mustard silk satin damask, matching that of a Newport wing chair which has been in the family for several generations. Another notable piece is a very fine English urn stand which is undoubtedly of museum quality, with its tripod base and gadroon-edged top. This pairs off very nicely with a George II (1740) tea table in walnut, with candle slides, and a writing chair in leather of the same date which, in turn, is quite at home with a pair of George I footstools of 1725, notable for their trifid feet and their period covering of red velvet.

There is also a ribbon-back armchair, dating from 1745, which has a needlepoint seat, and a mahogany desk of excellent proportions which originated in Scotland around 1770. In delightful contrast with these is a first quality Chinese painting (about 3 feet by 4 feet) done by an 18th century artist whose unusual medium, on the basis of stylistic evidence, was enamels. This depicts life in the East India Company compound of Macao.

The Dining Room, which also opens off the Hall, is rather more eclectic in style, combining Dutch,

ORIENTAL ROOM

The Oriental Room's most exciting piece is a rosewood altar table, seen at the left, of simple design with decorative brasses, dating from the Ming period. On it is a seven stringed Ming lute called a Chin, the type of instrument being played in a 15th century Chinese painting on the same wall.

Chinese, English, and Scottish items with those of America. Two of the walls in this room are sheathed and painted in a terra-cotta brown, the other two being plastered above the wooden dado. The window trim and the muntins are of the same color. An opening in one wall exposes a flight of black painted stairs leading to the second floor, while the windows, framed in sill length, self color draperies, look out upon the mill pond. The maize colored, white fringed rug was hand loomed in southern India especially for this room.

All of these details, however, are overshadowed by the dining table—a magnificent English made walnut piece dating from around 1650. The top is a single plank, 2½ inches thick, ten feet long, and 32 inches wide, as smooth as silk, and dark with age. The X-legs are extended into feet, the center stretcher supporting braces which rise to mid-length of the top for perfect rigidity. Down the middle of this table extends a Chinese runner of cut velvet in green and red. The six dining chairs—two of them with arms—are of the Charles II period with caned

171

MASTER BEDROOM

In the Master Bedroom one wall is sheathed, one paneled, two plastered, the wood being painted gray green, and there are five painted pine and maple chests. The portrait (which is of an unidentified gentleman) is attributed to Robert Feake.

seats and backs, the latter terminating in leaf crestings, all of fruitwood, japanned black in splendid contrast to their olive-green cushions.

Another fascinating piece in this room is a Dutch kas in miniature, which, though no more than two feet tall and two feet wide by fourteen inches deep, is so heavy as to be almost immovable single handed. The reason for this ponderosity is that the kas is made of lignum vitae, its double doors being two and one-half inches thick. Within it are two stacks of drawers topped by a shelf for hats. Paralleling one of the walls is a huge English bridal chest of yew (circa 1625-50), heavily carved and painted red, and ornamented with its handsome original lock and key of iron. On the front of this piece three family crests are carved and, by strange chance, inside the chest was found a document explaining the origin and significance of these crests. This chest serves to display a fine blue and white Ming bowl, dated 1605, and a pair of tall 17th century Scottish candlesticks in brass which are notable for their elegant proportions.

On the walls are two very fine Japanese two panel screens, dating from about 1650 yet in splendid condition. Both are of the Nagasaki school of painting, one depicting a Chinese trading vessel entering the harbor, and the other portraying a pair of foreign dogs of the whippet type much used in oriental design of the period and later. Both of these are in polychrome on a gold leaf background, and measure four feet by five feet, each being mounted in the traditional Japanese manner with a two inch brocade border in a lacquer frame. They are quite rare.

On the side of the house facing the water, the Summer Living Room has a window wall which provides a spectacular view over the mill race, pond, and dam, and their setting of huge rocks and overhanging elms. In this long room, which has a large brick fireplace at the outer end, informal early American furniture preponderates. Among these pieces is an early, and quite rare, Queen Anne armchair in cherry, still bearing much of its original paint. Other unusual chairs are a Tracy Windsor and a late 17th century Rhode Island banister back painted blue. The book-shelves hold an interesting collection of Toby jugs ranging in date from 1760 to 1790, some of them being the work of Ralph Wood, the others of the Astbury type.

A few other early American furniture pieces are found in the Master Bedroom where one wall is sheathed, another paneled, and two plastered. Both of the wood walls and the floor are painted in a gray green. In addition to a pine and cherry low bed, and a maple daybed, there are five painted pine and maple chests, with a Queen Anne looking-glass over the largest one. On the fireplace wall are two paintings, one an appealing portrait of a woman in 18th century garb, both the subject and the artist being unknown; the other a portrait of some unidentified gentleman which is attributed to Robert Feake.

The foregoing are the most used rooms in this unusual residence, and their contents indicate that, in spite of Mr. Ellsworth's major interest in oriental art, he is actually far more catholic in his tastes insofar as day-to-day living is concerned. Therefore, in order to avoid any suggestion of mere display in his living quarters, a special room has been set apart for the accommodation of his superlative collection of early Chinese furniture. This room is large, and filled with furniture in the taste of the intellectuals of the Ming ruling class. Basically simple in appearance, many of these pieces served several purposes. All of them are important, and some are actually the finest known of their type.

The room itself is simple, with white plastered walls, several windows with sill length curtains of a fabulous royal blue, and, at one end, an open stair to the upper floor, stained dark walnut. Undoubtedly the most exciting piece in this room is a beautifully grained rosewood sideboard—actually a family altar table used for domestic religious ceremonies in a Chinese home. Dating from the Ming period, it is 33 inches tall—the standard height for such pieces—

72 inches long, and 18 inches deep. As might be expected, the treatment is exquisitely simple, the only applied decorations being brass escutcheons of a typically oriental pattern. The pristine condition of this altar table, its owner points out, is due principally to the intense hardness and density of the wood—called by the Chinese "Hwang Hwa Li"—which even fire can scarcely mar.

This resistance to scarring and wear is also noticeable in a pair of late 16th century arm chairs of equally enchanting design. These have a gently curving splat back and a pillow roll which is said to have been the origin of the spoonback and neckrest in Queen Anne chairs of later years. These chairs have cushions in orange leather over the cane seats. Other pieces of equal note are two 17th century chests of camphorwood for clothing storage—usually silk garments lined with lamb's wool which the camphor fumes protect from insect damage.

Over the altar table is an extremely rare 17th century, Ming period rug in beige and blues, and, on its top, a pair of 17th century Chinese brass candlesticks stand guard over a seven stringed Ming lute called a Chin. In a 15th century painting on the same wall is portrayed a Chinese gentleman playing an instrument of the same type.

At one end of the room is a rare Chinese rosewood couch called a K'ang, standing about 18 inches high off the floor. It is covered with a mat and well supplied with cushions, and, with a canopy added, may be used as a bed. This example has a mat of leather, with cushions covered in the same material. Huge clothing chests ranged along one wall are of Chinese walnut, made in removable sections with smaller cupboards on top for hats.

Throughout this room are highly decorative Chinese garden seats of rosewood. These are quite rare, the tops being inlaid with Chinese marble, though probably not so hard to find as another *objet d'art* in this room—a stone carving of a bear, about ten inches tall, which once formed a leg of a sacrificial altar more than 1700 years ago.

THE TOWN HOUSE OF

Mr. and Mrs. David Stockwell, Antiquarians

DINING ROOM

The Chinese wall paper, visible through the open doorway of the Dining Room makes a striking background for the heirloom tall clock. On either side of the door is a corner cupboard displaying polychrome and white salt glaze stoneware, while centered on the Philadelphia Queen Anne walnut dining table is a Bristol delft bowl of 1740.

The dignified house that is the David Stockwells' family residence is modern in construction, yet almost Georgian in appearance, and therefore eminently suited to its 18th century interiors. Nestling in the shade of tall trees and hemmed in by yew hedges and flowering trees, it has an air of seclusion that is immediately dispelled on encountering its obviously hospitable portals. There is something inviting about the view through the glass enclosed vestibule that prepares one for the welcoming atmosphere of the wide Hall with its mustard trim and dado, its gay Chinese paper a riot of flowers, vines and tropical birds, a maze of pink, tan, and yellow against a background of rich green. Here are the tall grandfather clock, the Queen Anne chairs and marble topped table, all in well polished walnut, the ceiling sporting a three candle blown glass and gilt bronze lantern, and the floor adding its quota of

179

DINING ROOM

The dropped ceiling recess adding space to the Dining Room accommodates a dramatic oil painting and a pair of extra windows which help illuminate the rare Philadelphia Queen Anne chairs. The rug is a 17th century Oushak in red, blue, beige and pink.

luxury with the exotic colors and textures of oriental rugs. All these speak of a warm and comfortable home and welcome the stranger.

The rest of the rooms have the same inviting air, and the secret of it all undoubtedly is the obvious integrity of the whole; the absence of any false note or blatant anachronism to suggest that the house may not have gracefully matured over the past two

hundred years as it so obviously appears to have done.

Such an effect is not, of course secured gratuitously. It betrays an extensive knowledge on someone's part—an appreciation of old time furniture, and skill in the art of creating authentic backgrounds for fine antiques, plus the ability to select pieces which, though they may widely differ as to

180

DRAWING ROOM

Color is important here—off white ceiling and walls, wood in pewter green, old rose curtains and Herat and Feraghan rugs in blues, pinks and tans—a luxuriant foil for beige and coffee brocade of sofas and damask of chairs—matching the richness of polished walnut and mahogany.

age, provenance, and design, will yet remain wholly compatible. This further implies the ability to select wisely without succumbing to a pedantic consistency that makes a good museum but a monotonous home.

All of these things are evident in the Stockwell residence, as might be expected of a noted antiquarian, and most of the antiquities have been selected with a full knowledge of their origins and backgrounds. The Hall paper, for example, was made in China in the mid-18th century, and acquired from a house in Warwick, Long Island. The tall clock is a family heirloom. Its case was made by Nathaniel Dowdney in 1763, its works being supplied by Samuel Huston. Some of the Philadelphia Queen Anne chairs, dating from 1720-1730, were obtained from Graeme Park. Others, illustrated in the Blue Book of Philadelphia Furniture once belonged to the Gummere family, while the marble topped Queen Anne table with claw-and-ball feet—an early ex-

DRAWING ROOM

The major furniture pieces include two fine Chippendale sofas (one with the
Philadelphia ball and claw foot), a New England Marlborough legged sofa, a
Philadelphia lowboy with handled end panels, a Connecticut Queen Anne tea
table, a Philadelphia Pembroke table with block feet and other equally notable
Philadelphia and New England wing and open arm chairs—a collector's treas-
ure-trove.

ample of Dutch influence on New York design—
dates from around 1740 and came from Van Rens-
selaer Wyke. The Dining Room also is furnished
with Queen Anne period pieces against a background of off white ceiling and walls, with the trim,
dado, window bottoms, and pelmets in old mustard,
together with the pair of architectural corner cupboards, and the paneled doors opening into the Hall.
This room is particularly interesting for the rear ex-

tension which adds to it so much character as well as
extra floor space. This was effected by pushing back
the center part of the rear wall about five feet, making it possible to accommodate an extra window at
each side.

The dropped ceiling of this extension accommodates a pair of recessed lighting fixtures which provide illumination for the area after dark. A dramatic
note is added by a large, oblong oil painting—the

interior of a coffeehouse—the work of some 17th century Flemish or Dutch artist, which occupies most of the rear wall above the dado. The hangings here, as well as at the main windows are of off white linen, with borders and fringes of crewel work in muted tones. On the floor is a red bordered 17th century Oushak rug, patterned largely in blues, beige, and pink, a combination that adds a richness to the best of walnut furniture.

The dining table is a Philadelphia Queen Anne piece in walnut, dated about 1730 as duly recorded in the Blue Book of Philadelphia Furniture. Against the rear wall is a matching half of a similar table, flanked by Philadelphia Queen Anne chairs of an-

other Blue Book set. The marble topped table is New England Queen Anne of 1730 or so, and opposite this is a four drawer chest of Philadelphia provenance, and of about the same age. On the wall hangs a Queen Anne looking-glass with brass candle arms, and attached to opposite walls are two large and handsome lanterns which eliminate the need for a central chandelier. The Philadelphia Queen Anne walnut dining chairs have slip seats in pale yellow damask.

On both the marble topped table and the chest are displayed a number of collector's items, including 17th century Dutch silver candlesticks, and early 18th century American silver tankards. This brings

CORNER CABINETS

A corner cabinet and a hanging cupboard in the Drawing Room house collections of Chinese enamels painted with European figures and some dated Chinese Export porcelain.

BED PICTURE
In one of the bedrooms is this antique pencil post bed in authentic needlepoint
hangings embroidered by Mrs. Stockwell.

us to the important corner cupboards which are devoted to the display of polychrome and white salt-glaze stoneware of 1740-60. The only piece of pottery not included on these shelves is a large and extremely colorful Bristol delft bowl of 1740 which serves as a table center between meals.

In the Drawing Room the color scheme is changed somewhat, contrasting the off white ceiling and walls with a mantel, dado, and trim in pewter green. The mantel is a massive 18th-century Philadelphia piece with a gray marble facing and gouge work decoration, strongly architectural in design with its bold moldings. These latter complement the broad dado molding and the coved cornice which has a cross banded border. Balancing the heavy face of the mantel is a deep window valance of the same material as the curtains—a silk bourette in old rose. The Herat and Feraghan rugs have all over flower patterns in blues, pinks and tans, the pinks predominating to produce a warmly luxuriant effect that is a perfect foil for the beige and coffee brocade of the sofas, the damask of the chair seats, and the armchair upholstery, and matches the richness of the polished walnut and mahogany.

The major furniture pieces here include two fine Chippendale sofas. Of these one is of the Philadelphia ball-and-claw footed design of which only three others are known. The other, an heirloom, is a Marlboro legged sofa of New England provenance. There is also a Philadelphia lowboy with piecrust moldings, and carrying handles on the end panels, which is listed in the Blue Book as of 1760; a Connecticut Queen Anne tea table of the 1730s, with candle slides; a Philadelphia pembroke table with a scalloped top and Marlboro block feet; a Philadelphia Chippendale ball-and-claw footed wing chair of about 1776, and a 1750 Newburyport open arm chair with the same type of feet.

There are also a couple of Philadelphia chairs attributed to James Gillingham, and two corner chairs from the Philadelphia-New York area, circa 1730, not to mention a Blue Book pair of Marlboro legged, serpentine card tables, and two elaborately carved and parcel gilt mahogany looking-glasses of about 1760 which were found in the Philadelphia area.

Beneath the arm of the wing chair is a Pennsylvania spice cabinet, circa 1740, whose door is inlaid with a candlestick design and the initials of the original owner. Two architectural cupboards house collections of Chinese enamels painted with European figures, and some dated Chinese Export porcelain. The pictures likewise are of considerable interest, especially the set of six Chinese watercolors of Ports and Anchorages of the China Trade. Over the mantel is a portrait by Chinnery of a Chinese-American gentleman, and, above the lowboy, is a likeness of Peter Halcott by Alan Ramsay. On the sofa wall hangs a large landscape of "Richmond from One-tree Hill" painted by Reisbach about 1735.

Other details, such as the mantel garniture of gold-fish-scale Chinese Export lidded jars; a pair of rococo brass wall arms, and the several 17th century tall candlesticks (now electrified), are all in keeping with the general décor of what must be one of the most satisfying rooms in any present day American antiquarian's home where carefully scaled eclecticism is the order of the day.

ON LOYALTY FARM

The One-room Retreat of John W. Kluge, Connoisseur

190

INTERIORS

Interior of the log cabin chinked and whitewashed but hardly Spartan with its 17th century antique furniture pieces and lighting devices. The draw curtains are of a rich, dark blue, which, along with the Hamadan rug, supply a note of luxury. Wax candles provide the necessary lighting since no utilities are laid on.

On his thousand acre Virginia estate, John W. Kluge has both a mansion and an elaborate guest house with a pool pavilion. In addition, on a hilltop half a mile away, he has created a private retreat for himself, out of bounds to both family and guests. This novel and attractive—and somewhat romantic— hideaway is actually an ante-bellum log cabin, moved from its original site, with neither electricity nor water laid on, yet furnished with more valuable

and rare antiquities than many a full sized home. Here Mr. Kluge can rest in comfort—even luxury— and study, and contemplate.

With access to nowhere but the outdoors, the cabin offers its own private intimacy; it represents another and more remote world to which it is pleasantly possible to retire; an opportunity to detach oneself from the insistent immediacy of intruding things and people. It is an isolated place, pervaded

191

with a sense of the distant past, yet a calm and comfortable room which pays no tribute to clinical efficiency. In it, every item of furniture is intended to contribute to the mellow, quiet air, blending naturally with the rest so that the room can be appreciated as a whole, not merely as an assembly of related pieces which need to be examined and appraised individually.

It is a fairly big room as cottage or cabin rooms go, and full of interest but so different one cannot refrain from comparing it with all the others one has seen, being reminded that it is something intentionally different so that it cannot help evoking a mood

of solitude which all of us need at some time—some more often than others.

In furnishing the cabin, Mr. Kluge had the active cooperation of Mrs. Katharine Prentis Murphy, that dean of antiquarians, who selected the pieces out of half a century's experience in early Americana. Many of the items therefore date from the late 17th and early 18th centuries, all of them being of mint quality and largely of New England provenance.

The cabin itself is of squared cedar logs, chinked with oyster-shell mortar, its interior, including the board ceiling, painted white, the beams black, as is the battened door. Only the window frames and

muntins sport a dash of color—an antique brick red. The external chimney is a massive structure, incorporating a great stone fireplace with a twelve inch square wood lintel. Protecting the fireplace brickwork is a tombstone shaped castiron fireback, while jamb hinges support a long crane which would hold the heaviest of cooking pots, a service it is never likely to perform. The hearth is of brick, and the room floored with wide planks of hard pine.

At the windows are sill length draw curtains of heavy, fringed wool in a rich, dark blue. Interior lighting is supplied by a six branch, iron hoop type chandelier, given a modestly regal touch by a crown

shaped suspension ring, and by an adjustable twin candlestand, also of iron, a pair of brass wall sconces, and assorted brass candlesticks all of very early design.

On the hearth stands a firescreen composed of a medieval figure in colorful needlepoint, mounted on a cut out board with a heavy wooden base. Hung on the walls are a rack holding four churchwarden clay pipes, and an iron candlesnuffer—completing the list of practical accessories which add so much atmosphere.

Over the fireplace is an English royal coat of arms, carved in mahogany and emblazoned in muted col-

194

196

ors. The opposite wall, at the far end of the room, is dominated by a large portrait of Queen Elizabeth I of England—an oil painting thought to have once been much larger in size. This is mounted in a heavy eared and carved frame with heraldic sunflowers in the corners. Below this is a late 17th century oak chest with geometric panels and bun feet—a real museum piece, decorated with a pair of blue and white tobacco jars having brass covers.

Spaced around the room are four particularly fine banister back chairs—two side and two arm—by New Hampshire's John Gaines. These date from 1700 or earlier, and have tall, pierced crestings, turned legs, and pear feet, with loose seat cushions in blue calamanco to match the color of the curtains. A somewhat later banister back chair, long ago converted to a rocker (conducive to comfort and quiet thought!) has double-bearing arms and a splint seat.

In one corner of the room is a stunning little oak tavern table of 17th century New England. It has an oval top and beautifully turned legs, slightly splayed fore and aft, and tied together by substantial stretchers. Its top overhang is supported at the sides by a cleat notched into the apron. In the opposite corner is another table with a single drop leaf, slender turned legs with ball feet, and stretchers that seem too slight for tavern use. A third table is a gateleg in cherry, round topped, with two gates and nicely proportioned turnings.

There is also a low Queen Anne table with plain cabriole legs and a top inset with blue and white tiles. This fulfills the functions of a modern coffee table fronting a sofa which is in reality a bed, though of a particular sort. This, having a back, is more of a settle, and hardly seems wide enough to accommodate any but a child. In any event it is now used as a sofa, with heavy loose cushions in blue calamanco for both seat and back. It appears to be quite a late piece, of walnut painted black, and having turned legs and spindles. When it was first found there was a letter attached to it relating that is once belonged to a young girl in Virginia who, when she married, took it to Connecticut with her. Later, it was for some years used in a Connecticut church (doubtless *not* as a bed!), but now it is back in Virginia.

Among the smaller details that complete the furnishing of this room are an old New England corner shelf, and a larger wall shelf, both of pine, and a small looking glass with a wide and heavy frame. There are also several very interesting leather utensils—a wine flagon, such as soldiers carried, a half-gallon jack, and a wine bottle. Distributed among the tables and wall shelves are various sized horn tumblers, a silver mounted tiger ware jug, a blue and white china punchbowl, and several other pieces of pottery and porcelain as decorative items.

With these simple things the cabin has been transformed from a rude shelter to a useful adjunct to civilized living, as one is reminded by the colorful Hamadan rug of an oriental geometric pattern which seems perfectly at home upon the otherwise bare wood floor from which its origins are as remote as those of the cabin itself to its present use.

II

City Apartments

THE TOWN APARTMENT OF

Michael Greer, Interior Designer

TERRACE
Terrace of the Greer apartment at night.

BEDROOM

Mr. Greer's Bedroom emphasizes his interest in antique Steel pieces. The room
itself simulates a tent in beige silk, with an Empire Aubusson rug. The steel
bed is 74 inches long.

From the very fact of their compactness and limited
space, many town apartments pose decorating problems that are not ordinarily encountered in houses of
any size. For one thing, illumination by daylight is
likely to be restricted through fewer windows, and
lack of privacy where many and large ones are installed; for another, reduced room areas may mili-
tate against the use of bulky pieces of furniture.
Sometimes, too, problems arise concerning storage

space in the rooms themselves, with doors that need
to be transformed into part of the decoration or
otherwise disguised so that they do not simply constitute wasted wall area that prevents the proper
placement of furniture. On the other hand, one
normal advantage of such apartments is that the
ceilings usually are high, increasing the air space
but perhaps actually making the floor areas seem
smaller than they are—as well as necessitating a

205

FOYER

Papered walls with *trompe l'oeil* effect open up the Foyer to blue skies and a distant prospect.

FOYER STAIR

A carpet designed by Mr. Greer in pale gray with a classical border extends along the Foyer and up the Spiral Stair, giving an air of continuity to the decoration.

SALON

The Salon features Louis XVI and Directoire pieces in fruitwood and walnut, architectural interest being supplied by a statuary niche and pilaster-flanked doorway, and triple arches to the Dining Alcove.

longer and steeper staircase where two or more floors are involved.

In the apartment of Mr. Michael Greer, however, drawbacks such as these are handily overcome if not transformed into actual advantages, and there is nothing about any room that is in the slightest claustrophobic. Not only is the furniture of the proper scale, but advantage is taken of airy colors, mirrors,

and *trompe l'oeil* designs that introduce a feeling of spaciousness, in some instances opening the walls to what are apparently cheerful skies and distant prospects. This is particularly noticeable in the foyer where the papered walls represent arcades with topiary hedges and blue skies form the backdrop to exotic architecture fringed with Lombardy poplars in the misty distance. Below dado level are repre-

sented mossgrown walls; at the top a cornice is surmounted by decorative urns, the total effect being one of reducing the apparent height of the ceiling.

The two elaborate Empire six branch bronze chandeliers that illuminate the foyer are not only distinctive but unusual in that they are twins. On the floor is carpeting of a pale gray color with a classical border pattern in darker gray. This was designed by Mr. Greer himself, and continues on around the forty five degree turn of the hallway to

SALON
The Salon's only painted pieces—a cabinet displaying Creilware and other antique porcelains.

the spiral stair which it follows up to the second floor. In a semicircular recess at the bottom of the stair well stands a tall, carved and painted wooden gueridon serving as a pedestal for a terra cotta statue of a Roman goddess against the background of a garden wall provided by the foyer wallpaper.

From this point the stair rail ascends sharply in a graceful curve, upheld by slender, tapering round iron balusters shaped like delicate turnings—reminders of the fact that one of the owner's chief interests is metal furniture. Actually, he is the fortunate possessor of some of the finest examples extant, includ-

ing the work of early Renaissance French, English, and Spanish craftsmen who brought the art to perfection, a fashion to be revived by the French of the much later Louis XVI and Empire periods.

The most interesting group of these pieces is undoubtedly that found in Mr. Greer's bedroom. These range from a seventy four inch steel bed to a remarkable pierced and decorated inkstand that gleams like silver. This writing stand was presented by the citizens of St. Petersburg to the Empress Maria Feodorovna, in celebration of their defeat of Napoleon in 1814. The theme is a fountain and waterfall, with a winged centerpiece on a casket, four modeled figures and an urn at each corner, the whole mounted on feet representing highly detailed dolphins.

The bed is more practical than decorative, though it is also a work of art, and perfectly suited to modern use. There is also a fine steel side table with an amboina top and curule legs, the steel stretcher simulating a tapered turning, and the whole decorated with appropriate brass ferrules and caps. There is also a fascinating Louis XVI music stand that is a poem in wrought-iron and steel, yet intensely practical for its job. The desk is a Louis XVI mahogany *bureau-plat* with ormolu mounts, and there are also two round occasional tables of steel with tôle tops in bronze doré galleries. The four branch chandelier, equipped with glass dripcups, and a pair of antique table lamps, are all in tôle.

In other rooms are equally intriguing metalwork pieces—Directoire style painted sconces, tripod tables with pierced brass galleries and marble tops; Empire bronze tables; an ormolu Louis XVI marble topped table well adapted to bathroom use; a steel, folding campaign chair of the late 18th century with a velvet seat, and, most impressive of all, a leaden fountain complete with statuary which graces the garden balcony. In the foyer is a marble topped iron console, and metal bibelots galore throughout the rooms, the wonder of it all being that wood, fabric, and metal can, in capable hands, be made to seem so utterly compatible.

In the bedroom this is demonstrated in no uncertain manner, the interior being entirely lined with beige silk, framed in half-round molding painted black to simulate iron supports. The ceiling fabric is trimmed with a colorful braid patterned in a Roman design which extends from each corner to the center, giving the effect of a tent—a quaint yet interesting conceit that intrigued the Empress Josephine 150 years ago—a notion born of the military life that was in the forefront of so many minds in those martial days of conquest and revolution. Today the idea as interpreted by Mr. Greer smacks more of a cool retreat in the desert with every luxury at hand, and few reminders of the exigencies of modern civilization and everyday living.

As the owner has demonstrated, that idea can be pleasantly adapted to the confines of a cosy apartment, breathing of coolness, the light colors and fresh textures dramatized by the richness of woven braid, the upholstered, sound absorbing walls con-cealing storage spaces—the whole a fitting setting for the gilt bordered tôle and tooled leather, the tan ribbed velvet of the bed coverings, the gay orange, green, mauve, beige, and brown of an Empire Aubusson rug underfoot, and the Roman shades rising in artistic swags to let the pale morning light into this self contained cocoon.

Here there is also the patina and pattern of polished wood; the mahogany and leather of the huge desk top highlighted by pieces of crystal and polished marble obelisks so popular in the days of the Egyptian campaign, and the varied colors of a painted Directoire stool padded in tortoise-shell leather, and a pair of painted Empire fauteuils. On one side of the room ceiling-high storage cupboards are hidden behind the bordered fabric panels, the wall itself having formed upon it a pilaster that acts as disguise for a heating duct. Because of the storage spaces set out from the wall, the entrance to the bedroom is recessed, and twin doors are used so that when they are opened they do not project into the room beyond the closet walls. And even here the opportunity has not been lost to apply a further decorative touch by paneling the dropped ceiling within the door recess with pleated fabric bordered by the Roman braid.

The apartment's largest room is the second floor Salon where Louis XVI and Directoire pieces in fruitwood and walnut share honors with a painted cabinet whose curtain-edged, six-paned glass doors display fine, colorful examples of Creil ware and other choice specimens of antique porcelain. The room itself is given considerable architectural interest by a round topped alcove at the stair head which contains a three-quarter sized sculpture of a Roman goddess, illuminated by an ormolu and crystal chandelier hanging over the stair well, and by fluted pilasters, with paterae on the capital neckings, which flank the doorway to the kitchenette. The door trim and its six bold panels, plus a stunning high relief carving of fruit centered in the overdoor, together with the triple arches at the other end of the room, all combine to add a feeling of elegance to the Salon.

The height of the breakfront is balanced by a gilded and painted trumeau over the facing sofa in its gold damask; by a ceiling high gold framed mirror above an Empire console table; and by a tall, triple screen in pale green adorned with classic, grisaille figures, which stands between a grand piano and the wall. Beyond are the three archways, hung with pale yellow curtains and tasseled in terra cotta.

BEDROOM

The mahogany and leather of a huge Bedroom desk top displays pieces of crystal and polished marble obelisks and a tall tôle lamp highlighting an intricately beautiful steel inkstand that gleams like silver.

BATHROOM
The white "fabric" transforming this bathroom is actually a *trompe l'oeil* painting against gray walls.

KITCHEN

A tiny kitchen is given individuality by the color and form of architectural
surfaces, an eye catching Roman shade and a striking globular lighting fixture.

These open into a Dining Alcove whose french windows lead in turn to a tile floored balcony which seems ideal for summer dining when the striped and tasseled awning, like a medieval tent, is hung, and the tinkling fountain plays amid the potted shrubs and spindling palms.

In the alcove a delicate blue and white tôle chandelier sheds ample light on a circular Directoire marble topped pedestal table whose shaft, banded in gold, reproduces the delectable green of the leather loose cushions and arm pads of the Salon's cane backed Louis XVI beechwood armchairs. Lighting for this room is supplied by bronze sconces flanking the trumeau; by *bouillotte* lamps, by tôle table lamps and candlesticks, which fill it with a warm, mellow glow, augmented on occasion by a wood fire in the black marble fireplace.

Too small to be dignified by the appellation "Library" is the cosy little Book Room which offers both charm and comfort. It is furnished almost entirely in the Directoire style, including a settee and armchair, the wall between the two windows being occupied by a ceiling high painted bookcase displaying a collection of beautiful bindings. The windows are hung with translucent fabric, partially framed by lambrequins made from antique Louis XVI embroidered squares in green and red which look like ecclesiastical stoles. On the floor are two small Aubusson rugs, adding their quota of deep but subtle colors—wine, orange, and green—that add to the room's cheerful character. Perhaps the most striking piece—and the most interesting because of its association—is a deep Louis XV bergère which, together with its footstool, once belonged to Somerset Maugham. This bergère, with arms as high as the back, offers all the comfort and protection of a deep wing chair. In this room also is the folding iron campaign chair mentioned before.

Another point of interest in this apartment is the fact that extraordinary pains have been taken to make both the bathroom and the kitchen just as attractive as the other rooms, within their natural limitations. The bathroom in particular is a decorative triumph, the walls being covered with an astonishing example of *trompe-l'oeil* painting representing sheer white fabric stretched from cornice height to baseboard, and held by rings to metal rods top and bottom. The rods, in turn, are supported by what appear to be poles of round iron with decorative finials. The fabric seemingly is drawn outward at the center and held to the poles by pairs of large linked garlands. The total effect is highly dramatic against the pale gray walls, and reminiscent of the more formal tent effect secured in the bedroom.

Over the brass legged marble wash basin is a ceiling high, gold framed mirror, the basin itself having sufficient flat areas to accommodate a bronze bust and figurine, and an obelisk, beside the usual accessories. Even the wooden wall cabinet is given an architectural look, the mirror flanked by gold trimmed ebony pillars. Here, too, is the marble topped, iron based table already listed, with pictures and an elaborate wood carving above it. The bathroom lighting fixtures consist of a circular tôle hanging lamp, plus a hinged brass candelabrum either side the tall mirror. Even the light colored plastic tiled floor has been given added interest by an inlaid terra-cotta border whose lines terminate at the angles where they cross in decorative finials suggestive of iron strapwork.

The minuscule kitchen with its built-in oven, cabinets, and stainless steel sink, has been given a tremendous amount of individuality by outlining the doorways and panels in a dark green stripe, with diamond shaped figures in the cupboard panels. It also gains considerably from the globular hanging light fixture with its translucent globe, and the Roman shade over the french doors which open on to an iron railed balcony. The shade material has a pattern of leaves and fruit on a dark ground, the design being highly translucent and therefore extraordinarily decorative in the daylight—another point which serves to emphasize the importance of detail which has contributed so much to the perfection so obviously achieved in every phase of this apartment's décor and furnishing and added so much to its livability.

THE TOWN APARTMENT OF

J. A. Lloyd Hyde, Antiquarian and Collector

SALON

Mirror lined vitrines built into the salon walls display part of the Hyde collection of Peking enamels. The room walls are covered with an 18th century Chinese silk mural painting.

With two country houses as part time residences, J. A. Lloyd Hyde, noted authority on Oriental Lowestoft porcelain, has reserved for his town apartment the distinction of housing his fine collection of Peking enamels which is believed to be the world's largest, while totally avoiding any suggestion of a museum atmosphere. Fortunately, one room—the Salon—is of adequate size (18 by 30 feet) to permit the display of these treasures, and take full advantage of their decorative value without overpowering the rest of the furnishings, or having the room assume the aspect of a china shop as so many over enthusiastic collectors are apt to do. Instead, the display has become a natural part of the interior whose walls, from ceiling to dado, are enriched by an 18th century Chinese silk mural painting depicting scenes of court life in Jehol, North China, where the imperial household spent their summers centuries ago.

219

SALON

The focal point of one wall of the Salon is its greatest treasure—a 30 inch white enameled plate of 1770 showing the Emperor's children at play in the palace garden.

SALON
The three tall windows of the Salon are framed in valances and curtains in
gold silk with scarlet fringes and tassels.

Below the dado, a figured golden paper forms a tastefully plain background for the furniture pieces which are purposely restricted in height so as to minimize interference with the scenic wall covering, and eliminate competition with those *pièces de résistance,* the mirror lined vitrines built into the fireplace wall, and the colorful Peking Enamels they contain. The three tall windows of this room are framed in valances and curtains of gold silk in a chinoiserie design with scarlet fringes and tassels, the tops having tent like peaks in the manner of pagoda roofs.

At the opposite end of the room from the fireplace and vitrines is the greatest treasure of all—a thirty inch white enameled plate, made about 1770, on which is depicted a scene in pale blue, soft rose, and green, showing the emperor's children playing in the palace garden. This is hung at eye level, like a shining moon against the painted wall whose masses of green foliage might well be dark clouds floating in a sky of pure gold. This is truly the focal point of the room end, given weight by centering it over a Louis XV *bureau-plat* where a green shaded *bouillotte* lamp in ormolu shares a roseate embroidered bro-

221

BEDROOM

American Hepplewhite pieces grace the comparatively austere bachelor Bedroom. The bed is hung in dark blue "Tribute" silk with a beige pattern. The carpet is beige with striped borders in various hues of blue, relief being afforded by the yellow damask of the bench.

cade *tapis* with sundry pieces of decorative enamel and porcelain. Alongside this group is a particularly fine Louis XV chair in walnut, covered in gold brocade, which is signed by Nicolas Quinibert Foliot, official *menuisier* to the French royal household from 1749 on.

This grouping forms a perfect counterpoise to the facing fireplace wall, thus helping balance the entire room. In between the two are many interesting pieces of antique furniture, much of it in the Louis XV style, some quite modern but utterly compatible,

all tied together by a huge Kermanshah rug in muted colors which provides an ideal ground for the variegated upholstery and painted pieces.

One of the most unusual examples of enamel furniture is a Chinese low table which has narrow bandings of dark blue and red, and myriad tiny blue and pink flowers on a ground of the famed Manchu yellow so long reserved to the rulers of that dynasty. On a wall nearby is a fine and rather elaborate Louis Seize *cartel* in ormolu which has an extra large face and an urn finial.

DINING ROOM

An 18th century painted vitrine dominates the little Dining Room, its dark blue interior setting off a collection of Louis XVI Sèvres plates. A gold and white soup tureen of Oriental Lowestoft of considerable note is on the table.

Four cane backed side chairs with scarlet cushions; a pair of fauteuils in blue green brocade (circa 1760), and a large walnut *lit de repos à crosse* in green damask, with its accompanying pair of marble topped, red lacquer commodes, all add decisive touches of color, emphasizing the luxuriant atmosphere of this wholly sumptuous Salon. And a twelve branch chandelier in silvered glass casts a mellow golden glow over it all.

In such exotic surroundings those intriguing examples of the enameller's art displayed on the

vitrine shelves look their splendid best. Quite a few of them are unique, and therefore irreplaceable. Among such are the early teapots and kettles in European shapes though made in China; the platter covers bearing the arms of the Duke of Albuquerque; the inkstands and boxes decorated with red headed European personages; and the pair of lions on the mantelpiece.

In contrast with the Salon, the little Dining Room is classic in its simplicity. Designed for dining *à deux* —or, at most, *à quatre*—it still displays the hand of a sybarite or, at least, perfectionist. The walls and ceiling are of French gray, the cornice represented by a paper border of leaves and wheat sheaves in shades of blue green, the whole a perfect foil for the lambrequins and curtains of silver satin patterned in Chinese motifs and enlivened with a blue fringe. Under a delicate vase stemmed chandelier of Irish glass is a round extensible table, painted gray, and decorated in blue with husk swags and laurel wreath bands, as are the accompanying chairs, all products of the artistic genius of Jean Pillement.

Between the windows, facing the door to the Hallway, and towering above all else, is an 18th century painted vitrine with a provincial air. Its interior is a deep blue, against which a collection of Louis XVI Sèvres plates decorated with birds, together with a pair of China dogs and monkeys, stand out boldly. That blue is reflected in the taffeta seat cushions of the chairs. Between meals, the table is adorned with a gold and white soup tureen of Oriental Lowestoft (the subject of a color plate in the owner's work on Chinese Export Ware), flanked by ceramic candlesticks.

Still another decorative note is struck in the furnishing of the bachelor bedroom in this otherwise opulent apartment. Comparatively austere but perfection in actual quality, this other small room where the furniture setting is four light gray walls, a white ceiling and black baseboard, plus a beige carpet with striped borders in various tones of blue, the pieces themselves are American Hepplewhite in finely grained mahogany with no trace of inlay. The bed has reeded posts in the vase pattern, and a mahogany framed tester hung in dark blue "Tribute" silk with a beige pattern, and adorned with a fringe of the same tone—all matching the window draperies.

The neat bench at the foot of the bed is covered in contrasting yellow damask, adding a note of luxury. On the walls are hung a pair of family portraits in dull gilt frames, done about 1810 by John Vanderlyn in New York, and over the five drawer solid mahogany chest is a trumeau whose upper panel contains a pastoral scene painted in reverse on the glass in green and gold. Its architectural frame is flanked by wall sconces in Sheffield silver plate, elegant in their simplicity. On this chest stands a garniture consisting of three pieces of *blanc de Chine*—a representation of China's goddess of mercy, Kuan Yin, with wine cups on teakwood stands at either side—a delicate note on which to take leave of a warm and inviting group of interiors, each furnished according to its function, absorbing the display pieces as a necessary part of the general décor, with the accent on masculine taste and practicality as might be expected where the pride of a connoisseur is combined with the discipline of a professional interest in antiques.

THE TOWN APARTMENT OF

Mr. and Mrs. Harold W. Carhart, Collectors

226

DRAWING ROOM

Featured in the Drawing Room is this huge Chippendale breakfront displaying porcelain pieces, principally of the American Eagle pattern, against a background of celadon damask.

The display of a large collection of antique porcelains in traditional surroundings may present certain difficulties to the decorator, but in their city apartment, Mr. and Mrs. Harold W. Carhart, have solved the major problems handsomely. Here they have successfully combined comfortable modern furniture with handsome 18th century antiques, providing room for spacious modern living against sympathetic backgrounds throughout which the collection is judiciously distributed. The result is a group of interiors in which the method of display is adapted to the variation in formality that each room represents. In other words, the pieces forming the collection are treated according to their degree of adaptability to grouping as well as their individual decorative value and antiquarian interest.

Thanks to this selective treatment which utilizes extensive aggregations as well as single units, and a

227

THE DESK
The desk pigeonholes are devoted to the display of cups, boxes and coffee pots.

DINING ROOM

In the Dining Room, a breakfront vitrine contains one of the finest collections of Chinese porcelains with New York State coat of arms, a Compagnie des Indes tray and a noted set with American Eagle decoration and motto.

basic furnishing plan which mixes 20th century upholstered seating and modern fabrics with classical antiques while providing ample room for circulation, the current ideal of space and serenity has been felicitously achieved. Each room accommodates units of the collection which have been incorporated into the general décor in such a manner as to avoid detracting from either, achieving a certain dignity without excessive formality. In this way the maximum decorative value of the porcelains has been maintained without displaying large numbers of them on every wall, table, or mantelpiece, or overaccenting the displays so that they overpower the rest of the furnishings, or emphasize the contrasts between modern pieces and the antique treasures.

This in itself represents an admirable *tour de force* which reveals both the personality and the sure taste of the owners who have successfully avoided any suggestion of clutter by limiting wall decorations, such as pictures, to a minimum, giving pride of place to the collection which is of necessity composed of things related both in scale and spirit.

229

It is these relationships between the groups and between the separate pieces that extend their interest by providing comparisons and emphasizing differences. The total display in any one room therefore has a greater dynamic appeal, and far stronger emphasis than dozens of scattered pieces possibly could have.

Obviously this applies principally to items that have something in common such as a color, design, or surface pattern so that the individual piece needs no further investigation or identification. The only possible exceptions are three dimensional pieces such as jugs and vases which usually need to be seen in the round in order to be analyzed and fully enjoyed. This means that each of them is best isolated and shown separately, gaining importance in the process. Both of these methods have been used with great success in the Carhart apartment. In the Drawing and Dining Rooms, for example, large groups of porcelains have been confined to handsome and massive, glass-fronted furniture pieces which serve much the same function as frames to paintings, circumscribing the groups and displaying related pieces as a unit, while isolating the whole from other decorative features of the rooms. In other places, such as the Library, individual pieces—mostly those that can stand alone and need to be seen in the round in order to be fully appreciated—are distributed as accents in locations where they prove the most effective.

The Chinese Export Porcelain (commonly referred to as Chinese Lowestoft) owned by Mr. and Mrs. Carhart actually forms one of the most important collections from the standpoint of both variety and quality. Much of this ware was brought from Canton to American east coast ports between 1783 and 1815, the decorations ranging from the coat of arms of the United States to the eagle and monogram designs, while some had nothing more than the bird and a few flowers in the central shield.

In the beginning, the Chinese porcelain decorators copied the Great Seal of the United States almost exactly, the eagle having an olive branch in one talon, a sheaf of arrows in the other, and the motto: *E Pluribus Unum* below. With the passage of time many curious and fascinating variations of the original came to be painted on tea sets, punchbowls, covered cups, dining services, and vases. In all instances the ware itself is white, off white, or grisaille, and the principal colors used in its decoration are sepia and orange, blue, and gold. Examples of several varieties are included in this collection.

In the Drawing Room the furniture pieces are dominated by a huge mahogany Chippendale breakfront cabinet incorporating a desk. This is flanked by a pair of English Sheraton wheelback chairs. At one end of the sofa which is placed along the adjacent wall is a Chippendale tea table with a scalloped top; at the other end is an octagonal one. In between is a Chinese Chippendale coffee table. Other mahogany pieces consist of a pembroke table, a miniature chest serving as end table to the loveseat, and a fireplace bench upholstered in red velvet which provides a welcome spot of color. These all stand out against the pale blue of the walls and trim, the creamy tint of the draperies enlivened by fringes and tassels in beige and blue, and by the cream damask of the upholstered pieces on a rug of pale gold. No other accents are needed.

Since the four breakfront doors are of glass, a large number of porcelain pieces are visible on the celadon damask lined shelves. The pieces actually comprise a superb collection of the American Eagle pattern porcelains, including a plate with the spread eagle, cluster of flags, cannons, and so on, which has a border in sepia and orange. There is also a set of twelve small, covered pots bearing the United States arms, with orange borders; a dinner plate used by George Washington at Mount Vernon which is decorated with the device of the Society of the Cincinnati; and a pair of orange bordered Fitzhugh 16 inch platters, their centers inscribed: "R. Smith, Mississippi." The desk pigeonholes are occupied by two sets of Chinese style cups, an assortment of porcelain boxes, and a pair of coffee pots. On the scalloped table is displayed alone a Lowestoft plate from the service which Louis XV presented to Madame de Pompadour, while less important examples of the ware form the mantel garniture and decorate the small tables.

Somewhat more austere is the Dining Room in which large expanses of bare white wall give added importance to a wide breakfront cabinet or vitrine; the handsome inlaid Sheraton sideboard facing it, and the set of nine mahogany Connecticut urn backed chairs which date from 1790 and are upholstered in off white silk with a green stencil design. In the center of the pale gold sculptured rug stands an oversized mahogany drop leaf dining table, with an early and quite rare Lowestoft tureen in underglaze blue and gold centered upon it. Over this hangs a delicately beautiful crystal and ormolu chandelier.

On the sideboard are some of the rarest pieces of Chinese Lowestoft in this collection—a punchbowl

LIBRARY

The gaily decorated Library in china blue English chintz is host to a rare Chinese porcelain plate dated 1783. The books are interspersed with jugs, cups, saucers, bowls and a teapot. On the mantelpiece are plates, cups and saucers in grisaille.

of 1731 with the arms of the Peers family of England repeated five times on its outer surface; an armorial platter, and a number of melon shaped pieces decorated with the coat of arms of Denmark and the representation of a ship.

The great cabinet, centered on one of the long walls, is devoted to the display of one of the finest and most complete collections of Chinese porcelains extant bearing varied representations of the coat of arms of New York State. Here also is an extremely rare rectangular porcelain tray in blue and gold,

with the arms of the *Compagnie des Indes*, and a well-known set with an American eagle decoration and the motto: "In God We Hope."

Gayest of the three principal rooms displaying the porcelains is the somewhat less formal, smaller and cosier Library, dazzling with its white walls and ceiling, its draperies, pelmets, and upholstery in a China blue English chintz which sports sprays of flowers in yellow, white, and dark blue. The furniture here, too, is of mahogany, including a brass bound low table before the sofa, ingeniously con-

231

trived from an old gun case, and a tall William and Mary desk between the windows on which stands a rare Chinese porcelain platter dated 1783 and bearing the arms of an Irish regiment.

At one end of the room are bookshelves crowded with handsomely bound volumes which make room here and there for china jugs and a row or two of colorful porcelain cups and saucers, bowls, and a teapot. On the mantel are plates, cups and saucers in grisaille, decorated with scenes from "The Fishing Lady" series, each mounted on its little mahogany stand. Few of these items however can compare for interest with the set of eight gold-framed watercolors by the famed English painter, J. M. W. Turner, in which Mr. Carhart takes a particular pride.

All in all, it might be said that as backgrounds for the collection the rooms lose none of their individuality, catering to the owners' tastes as to style, mood, and color; combining modest formality with elegance into which the porcelains introduce a note of diverse delight. And who could ask for more?

THE PENTHOUSE OF

Churchill J. Brazelton, Antiquarian

234

A penthouse with a roof garden on three sides as a rule offers splendid opportunities for the creation of an air of sequestration having little cognizance of the teeming city below, and that of Churchill J. Brazelton is no exception. It does, in fact, go much further than most because of Mr. Brazelton's taste for the exotic and his familiarity with the art and artifacts of the ancient world. These are the reason why his terraces are as fascinating as his interiors,

and can be enjoyed the year round thanks to the statuary and plantings no less than the oversized windows which give on to them.

At one corner of the tile floored terrace is a tiny *pavillon* of classical design with a round, marble topped table of ram's head design suggestive of ancient Rome. In other corners are brick planters, with wooden ones and tall urns spaced along the walls and parapet, all crowded with flowering bushes and

SALON

Striated green velvet walls, rich warm faïences, and antique pieces of Louis XIV, XV and XVI periods create a room of unparalled richness in which a huge Brussels tapestry seems perfectly at home.

trees of exuberant foliage. Interspersed are white marble columns and statuary pieces, a marble and bronze well head, an armillary sphere in bronze, and a brick based fountain surmounted by a life sized white marble Venus de Medici set in an archway of trellis that isolates it from its background of tall buildings. The furniture is all of iron—cast and wrought—painted white, with glass topped tables, and chairs and sofa with cushions in gay colors—the

whole as remote from a modern metropolis as a garden in Aulis.

Looking out into much of this is the many windowed Salon which is just as sumptuous with its walls of striated green velvet and rich furnishings of the Louis XIV, XV, and XVI periods. In accord with the owner's conviction that it is a mistake to employ only pale colors in such rooms, the fabrics are of rich and warm hues (many of them XVIIIth century),

only the ceiling being off white to make the most of the lighting whether natural or artificial. What little trim is visible is marbleized in black and white for contrast, the draperies a gold Fortuny print, the rug a neutral beige. One wall, however, is almost totally covered by a huge Brussels tapestry made by the "Meister" Marcus de Vos, in about 1720. This is executed to a reduced scale so that the figures are smaller than usual, giving extraordinary depth to a landscape which depicts a variety of rural activities (including tender dalliance!) during autumn months.

This is a very large room and contains a great deal of furniture, as was customary in the 17th and 18th centuries. From the ceiling's center hangs a huge crystal and ormolu chandelier with large crystal bull's eyes set in the ormolu crown—a historic piece presented by Napoleon to the Burgundy family. On the fireplace wall is a Louis XV marble mantel in two tones of brown, and over this a sectional mirror bordered by Louis XV pilasters extends to the ceiling, covering the entire chimney breast. In the center of this mirrored surface a large 18th century *cartel* in ormolu gleams like an oversized jewel, competing for attention with a pair of tall and elaborate marble and crystal candelabra.

With so much furniture the groupings need to be carefully balanced both as to textures and colors to

ENTRANCE HALL

In the tiny Entrance Hall the richness of the Great Salon is suggested by the
same velvet wall covering, one section covered with mirror squares reflecting an
elaborate rock-crystal and gilt bronze Louis XV chandelier.

maintain an air of order. This has been skillfully
done. The principal seating piece is a huge sofa in
cream silk damask which stands beneath the tapestry. At one end is a carved and gilt Louis XV table
with a gray and brown marble top on which rests a
beautiful Louis XVI urn shaped lamp in ormolu and
marble. Towering above it is a ten foot Roman col-
umn of brown marble supporting a wide and shallow porphyry Louis XIV urn.

At the other end of the sofa is an extremely rare
table of ebony with a boule top, bronze mounts and
a carved shell border in bronze doré around the edge
of the top. Dated as of 1740, this piece is signed by its
maker, Philippe-Claude Montigny, one of the best
cabinetmakers of his generation. It has a tortoise-
shell inlay of a distinctly red tone, and is similar to a
number of such tables found in the Palace of Versailles.

In front of these is a pair of Louis XV gilt chairs in antique cream silk, while twin marble topped low tables separate the sofa from a banquette in crushed strawberry silk patterned in tan, green, and delicate blue. This is reinforced by a pair of Régence bergères in fruitwood covered in the same material, one on either side of the fireplace so that all supply decisive masses of color in the midst of which is a Louis XVI gilt fireside stool in a heavenly light blue velvet.

On the far side of the room, under the great window, is a Louis XVI loveseat in olive green velvet behind which, on the window sill, is a pair of white marble sculptures by Bernini (1598-1680). Between this and the fireplace wall stands a large circular

table covered with a sumptuous antique silk cloth embroidered in a delicate floral pattern and edged with a multicolored fringe which was made for it in France. On this table a lamp with a colorful base of blue john and ormolu casts a mellow glow upon a fascinating collection of *objets d'art* from many parts of the world.

Flanking the large window is a pair of fine English sconces of 1780 in gilt wood, one carved to represent "The Arts," the other "Agriculture." One of these helps to illuminate a rare and valuable *bureau-plat* —another Montigny piece—which has its original, silver bordered black leather top. The wood is bleached and black ebony with silver inlay, the

239

240

mounts, escutcheons, and hoof feet also being of silver. On this table are many small items of vertu. The vase and pedestal lamp base is of blue john with ormolu mounts, and also on the table are a pair of ormolu trimmed white marble obelisks, a pair of silver sphinxes, one with the bust of Madame Du Barry, the other representing Madame de Pompadour; two Louis XVI candlesticks, an ormolu inkstand and tray, and similar treasures, all adding to the overall atmosphere of refined taste. Actually, these bibelots constitute a collection in themselves. The accompanying *fauteuil de bureau* has its original upholstery in deep gold with a pattern in blues and reds.

On the wall above this table is a portrait of one of Napoleon's favorite generals, the Duc d'Abrantès, better known as Maréchal Junot. This was painted by the Baron Jean-Antoine Gros (1771-1833).

Close by the entrance to the Salon is a three-drawer commode in black lacquer with bronze escutcheons and handles which is signed by Hache. This forms the base of an attractive grouping. On it is a pair of Louis XVI marble and ormolu candelabra which serve to illuminate a portrait of the same vintage by an unknown artist, the subject being an equally unidentifiable boy. Over the picture is arranged a carved wood swag, and under it is an English epergne in silver gilt, dated 1772. On special occasions this is adorned with colorful fruit, from a pineapple to luscious purple grapes, thus completing an ensemble *tres ravissante*. On either side the commode is a Louis XV chair with a low, wide seat in its original gray silk upholstery with touches of blue, tan, and green embroidery.

A similar impression of luxurious furnishing is conveyed by the Foyer which has the same velvet covered walls except for that facing the entrance door which is mirrored. From the ceiling hangs a large rock-crystal and gilt bronze Louis XV chandelier with an urn stem and ball drop. Fortunately this, when illuminated as it must be most of the time, is only partially reflected in the semi-opaque and very, very old mirror sections forming the wall surface. The woodwork here too is marbleized in black and white, and the floor is of black linoleum with white striping, and against this neutral background the furniture pieces look their charming best.

These pieces consist of a pair of exceptionally fine carved beechwood armchairs with cane backs, partially covered in pale blue velvet, and with cushions of the same material. Opposite these is a gold mounted commode in black enamel, having floral panels in color, over which hangs a carved and gilded Louis XVI mirror with the stamp of the Chateau of Versailles. A pair of white alabaster and ormolu candelabra provide the local illumination.

In a corner by the Salon entrance is a round table with a cover of cut velvet in dark blue on a neutral ground. On this stands a gilt *bouillotte* lamp and several small decorative objects from the major collection. Other features are a small Louis XV *cartel d'alcove*, sconces, an oil painting, and two Chinese painted mirrors in gilt rococo frames.

As usual in such apartments, the bedroom has little in common with the more public rooms. Nevertheless, though restrained in color and decoration, it teems with interest. The walls are covered in scarlet faille, hand applied by a French craftsman. The ceiling is tan with a narrow Roman key border, top and bottom, in black and white. This pattern is repeated in the otherwise plain bedspread whose color matches that of the walls. The rug is modern and dark blue in color.

This room has a totally military aspect, reflecting the owner's interest in his Napoleonic collection of oil paintings, uniform decorations, swords, emblems, medallions, proclamations, et cetera which cover the walls. Dominating the room is the Directoire chandelier in black and gold tôle, complete with its thirty-inch blown-glass drip pan which has some of the effect of a huge lens. Another outstanding piece is an ebony table with ormolu mounts by Guillaume Benneman, made during the reign of Louis XVI. This vies for attention with a fascinating mahogany Directoire chair with an Egyptian air which is signed by Georges Jacob (1739-1814). This has a lotus leaf back in carved wood independent of the arms which, together with the seat, are covered in olive green leather, and brass nailed. Its legs are tapered and reeded.

There are many other notable pieces in this room which, like the rest of the apartment, suggests years of knowledgable collecting, the whole being somewhat reminiscent of John Singer Sargent's memorable painting, "Venetian Interior" and every bit as imaginative and atmospheric.

THE TOWN APARTMENT OF

Elmo D. Avet, Antiquarian and Interior Designer

244

LIVING ROOM

The Avet Living Room combines a variety of compatible objects from East and West such as life size figures of Cambodian warriors, Venetian lanterns, a polar bear skin, and pink upholstered chairs, resulting in whimsical splendor with plenty of gold accents, mother-of-pearl and black lacquer, set off by room high draperies in vivid grays topped by pelmets of gleaming brass.

A study of the highly personal and unusual apartment which Elmo Avet has created for himself is a lesson in geography since a round dozen countries—from Scotland to India—supplied the furniture, paintings and accessories in what must be the most individual and original set of interiors ever devised by an antiquarian of world wide experience.

Born in Louisiana of French and Corsican parentage, Mr. Avet spent many years in the markets of Europe and Asia in search of the exotic and the unusual. The apartment he has recently completed represents some of the fruits of that odyssey. Its contents are rare, different, and nostalgic, and at the same time beautiful regardless of current fashion and modern taste.

His scheme for one of his most important interiors —that of the Living Room—was to combine a variety of compatible objects from East and West, even

BEDROOM

Inspired by turn-of-the-century rooms at Shepheard's Hotel, Cairo, the principal Bedroom combines the exotic with richness and dignity, utilizing bamboo, lavender Thai silk, leopard skin, pierced teak furniture painted white, and a Chinese *blanc de Chine* dancing girl. In the midst of all this is a fine set of French prints entitled "The Four Seasons" dating between 1810 and 1820.

utilizing some whose affinities were not immediately obvious, such as a tremendous white polar bear skin rug with a three drawer black and gold commode decorated with metal monkeys and acorn drops.

Perhaps the most striking feature of this room, however, is the off white window wall, its tall, narrow chimney breast supporting a pair of white painted, life sized figures of Cambodian warriors armed with ivory elephant tusks. This is hemmed in by ceiling high, lush and voluminous, window draperies in a large and bold pattern of two tone gray, topped by deep silken swags under repoussé brass pelmets that sparkle like bright gold. In contrast, the tiny Louisiana fireplace in white painted cast iron is insignificant yet succeeds in adding its quota of beauty.

Another exotic touch is supplied by a massive Venetian lantern of plate glass and punched metal that might well have come from some Italian pa-

lazzo. Contributing to the whimsical splendor of this interior is the bright pink silk of the upholstered chairs, the sofa and fireside stool which is picked up by the marbleized lampshades and repeated in the diaper patterns of the backs and seats of a pair of Louis XV fauteuils. To this is added the splendor of a tall triple French screen, carved and gilded, each panel composed of three sections of frosted glass with a transparent design.

Other gold accents are provided by the narrow frame of one tall oil painting, the gilt chair frames, the gold decorated commode, and a number of metal bibelots distributed around the room. To these may be added the bright touches of mother-of-pearl inlay of several black lacquered teakwood stands and one

of the other real "objects of art"—a carved teakwood table whose glass top reveals a display of beautifully carved flowers in mother-of-pearl and ivory.

All of these are unobtrusively tied together by a room size modern rug in a warm gray which serves as a perfect foil for the deep pink, and emphasizes the deeper grays of the hangings and the yellowish white of the skin rug with the black and gold of the furniture pieces and the large areas of off white represented by the walls and ceiling. The total effect is one of a brilliant interior that is lively without being restless, gay and unusual yet far from garish.

Something of the same verve and esprit is apparent in the bedroom which has been designed to recapture the manner and period—at the turn of the

247

THE STUDY

A room of mementoes is the Study—containing an amazing aggregation of memorabilia from a painting of the owner as a young man to a fantastic sofa of buffalo horns upholstered in antelope skin; from a painting of Mary, Queen of Scots, to a table whose base is a life size bull's head in blue and gold, once a French *boucherie* sign!

century—of the world famed Shepheard's Hotel in Cairo. This room, too, is utterly "different," providing a rare combination of the exotic with richness and dignity. The high ceilings of these rooms undoubtedly have much to do with the last-named quality—or attitude. This is exemplified by the four tall windows with their stately hangings of exquisite Thai silk in a deep lavender with fringes and cords of a darker hue. The handsome pelmets above them, with their delicate moldings, are of wood painted

white, with central carved masks designed to hold the cord swags in the middle. Against the white walls the impact of these vivid masses of color is tremendous, quite apart from the effect produced by the use of this same color in the coverlet of the bed and the upholstery of the banquette at the foot of it.

The bed itself is of simulated bamboo, painted a pale yellow as are the tall shelves and table alongside it. The bamboo motif is also applied to a small occasional table, and to a desk which has a panel inset with leopard skin. Such color, texture, and openwork design seem particularly suited to a warm climate, as might be expected considering the origin of the pieces. The rest of the furniture also is of a type rarely seen in this country. Made in India from solid teak it is pierced and carved then painted white so that its surface looks more like lace than wood. It is, however, quite heavy and substantial, even the scalloped edges of the circular pedestal table, and the leafy projections of a chair seat apron being far from fragile.

One exception to the lacy style is a massive sofa carved and painted in an openwork design of vines, birds, animals, and human figures so that it looks like cast iron. Another extraordinary piece is a ten sided pedestal table with three feet, every part of which is deeply carved in an over all leaf pattern. On this stands an Indian carved wood figure. On the round table is a Chinese goddess, two feet high, in *blanc de Chine*. The most interesting decorative feature, however, is probably a wall bracket of carved wood, softly gilt, its design based on the figure of an Indian dancing girl. This hangs high on a wall between two windows, where it supports a tall, slender necked brass vase from which springs an even taller spray of flowers and foliage, wonderfully constructed of wire and colored beads in shaded purples and reds.

Over the bed is a framed floral design in needlepoint, and on the floor a leopard skin with a mounted head threatens the sleepwalker with disaster. The only other artwork consists of a fine set of French prints entitled "The Four Seasons." These were printed sometime between 1810 and 1820.

Taken together, these two rooms suggest the ultimate in imaginative design, and after savoring their exotic formality one is scarcely prepared for the third room of this suite which presents the ultimate in bohemian unconventionality. This is the Study—a room of memories and mementoes, floored with parquet and sheathed in white painted paneling with a white ceiling and trim as a background for an amazing aggregation of memorabilia from a painting of its designer as a young man to the African weapons and zebra skin rug. Africa also is represented by the fantastic sofa of buffalo horns upholstered in antelope skin, once the property of the late Kurt Weill, the noted German born American composer. There is also a pair of horn legged lamp stands, the lamps being composed of beautifully modeled Samoan dancing girls with fantastic headdresses.

Two of the chairs which have round backs, sloping arms and curule legs were made in China for the Austrian trade. Beside these the daybed is almost commonplace, being nothing more than a provincial Louisiana sleigh bed in mahogany. The great desk, on the other hand, is an early 19th century Dutch piece, painted *faux-bois* over pine, and crammed with secret compartments. Nearby stands a low table with a circular top of heavy plate glass, its base a life size bull's head in blue and gold that once was a French *boucherie* sign!

All these things contrast strangely with a large oil painting of Mary, Queen of Scots, and her young son who was destined to become James I of England. Though the artist is not known, this picture is definitely of the period, though the frame is not.

On the walls, ledges, and brackets of this remarkable room are busts, sculptures, bronzes, a collection of African tribal weapons, valuable porcelain bowls, a knight's breastplate which serves to conceal a wall light, and a death mask of Napoleon. Radiance is shed upon this weird mélange by a four branch chandelier of polished brass that can only have come from some Parisian bistro, with which legendary city its affable owner has more than a nodding acquaintance—and some enviable souvenirs.

GLOSSARY

A

ADAM, ROBERT (1728-92): Noted English architect, who also created new forms of furniture design.

AGATE WARE: A veined and mottled pottery resembling agate in appearance.

APPLIQUÉS: Wall sconces, usually with two or three candle holders or branches.

ARMOIRE: A storage cupboard for clothing, originally devised for armor.

ASTBURY, JOHN (1686-1743): English producer of a lead glazed earthenware decorated with applied reliefs.

AUBERGINE: A purple enamel or glaze used first in Chinese ceramics during the Ming dynasty.

AUBUSSON: Fine French hand woven tapestries; originally used as wall hangings but now in great demand as rugs. Usually square and very large.

B

BACCARAT CRYSTAL: High grade glass produced at Baccarat, France, beginning in 1818.

BAIL HANDLE: Semi-circular or curved drawer handle.

BANISTER BACK: A chair back formed with vertical turned spindles or such spindles split into two down the center.

BANQUETTE: A French term for a long stool or settee without arms or back.

BEAUVAIS TAPESTRY: Fine French tapestry produced at Beauvais, near Paris, from 1664 on.

BELL POTTERY: The so-called Shenandoah Valley pottery—redware and stoneware—made by Solomon, Samuel or Peter Bell from the 1820s to the 1880s.

BELL AND HUSK INLAY: Decorative inserts on fine furniture, much used by Adam and Hepplewhite.

BENEMAN, GUILLAUME: 18th century designer of fine French furniture, of German origin. Principal cabinet-maker to the Court of Louis XVI from the late 1780s on.

BERGÈRE: A French armchair with upholstered sides and a loose cushion.

BERNINI, GIOVANNI L. (1598-1680): Italian painter, sculptor, and architect.

BIBELOT: Any small decorative article of charm or value.

BIRD CAGE TABLE: A table embodying a cage like structural feature which permits the top to tilt and turn.

BLACKAMOOR: English term applied to guéridon or candlestand in the form of a negro figure, originating in France.

BLANC DE CHINE: An all white Chinese porcelain first made during the Ming period, and called, in Chinese, Chien Yao.

BLUE JOHN: A variety of colored fluorspar found in Derbyshire, England, used in making vases and ornamental pieces.

BOBÊCHE: A saucer shaped disk which fits on to a candleholder to catch wax.

BOISERIE: The wood paneling of rooms.

BOKHARA RUG: An Oriental rug originating in Turkestan.

BOLECTION MOLDING: A molding which projects beyond the surface of a panel, or connects two surface levels.

BONNET TOP: The scrolled top of an American Queen Anne style highboy or chest-on-chest.

BOUCHERIE: Wood decorated by impregnating with copper sulphate—an invention of Francis Boucher (1703-1770).

BOUILLOTTE: A French game.

BOUILLOTTE LAMP: A French table lamp of bronze doré.

BOUILLOTTE TABLE: A circular table with a gallery to retain a removable cover for the marble top when playing the game of bouillotte.

BOURETTE: A fabric woven from knotty floss so that the knots form an interesting texture or pattern.

BRISTOL WARE: English delftware made in Bristol in the 18th C.

BRONZE DORÉ: Gilded bronze.

BROWN, WILLIAM HENRY: Noted 19th century silhouettist.

BUN FOOT: A flattened, circular ball foot introduced in the last half of the 17th century.

BUREAU-PLAT: A flat writing table or desk, usually with drawers.

BUREAU EN DOS D'ANE: A French drop leaf desk (supposed to be the shape of an ass's back).

C

CACHEPOT: A decorative flower pot holder of porcelain, tôle, or other material.

CALAMANCO: A glossy, woolen material made in England and Flanders, having checks visible on one side only due to the method of weaving.

CANAPÉ: A sofa.

CANDLE SLIDE: A small wooden shelf made to slide out from under a table top.

CARLTON HOUSE DESK: A large English writing desk of the late 18th century, consisting of a three drawer table with a curving group of small drawers above.

CARTEL: A French wall clock.

CAUDLE CUP: A two handled cup, usually with a cover, in which caudle (a warm drink of gruel and wine) was served.

CELADON: A sea green, translucent glaze imitating jade, associated with Chinese porcelain.

CELLARET: A lead lined wooden stand to hold wine bottles in the dining room.

CHARGER: A large china or silver plate to hold a joint of meat.

CHELSEA WARE: Porcelain made in Chelsea, England from about 1745 to 1784.

CHENETS: French andirons.

CHINESE EXPORT PORCELAIN: The same as Chinese Lowestoft, q.v.

CHINESE GARDEN SEATS: Ornamental, barrel shaped seats about 2 feet high made of teakwood or porcelain.

CHINESE LOWESTOFT: Is a hard paste porcelain made and decorated in China for export to foreign countries.

CHINOISERIE: A term used for items made in Europe in the Chinese style or inspiration. It is not applied to anything produced in China itself.

CHIPPENDALE, CHINESE: Furniture designed by Chippendale in the Chinese style of simulated bamboo or lattice work.

CHIPPENDALE, PHILADELPHIA: Georgian style furniture made in Philadelphia.

CHUTES: Applied, protective decorations of bronze on angles and legs of French furniture from Louis XIV period.

CLOISONNÉ: A method of decorating metal ornaments with enamel, employing wires to separate sections containing the various colored enamels.

COMMODE: A French type chest of drawers, frequently decorated with ormolu mounts and a marble top.

COMPASS DESIGN: Any decorative design that can be made with a pair of compasses.

CONSOLE: A decorative table used against a wall, supported by one or more brackets or consoles.

COROMANDEL WOOD: A decorative striped ebony from the Coromandel coast of East India.

COROMANDEL LACQUER: Used on Chinese screens. It consists of several coats of a paint made from a tree sap colored with pigments, such as cinnabar (red). Often in layers of different colors, exposed by incising the design.

CRANE: An iron bar attached to a wall hinge in an Early American fireplace on which pots may be hung.

CREIL WARE: A French, transfer printed, tin glaze ware of the 18th and 19th centuries.

CRESTING: Decorative carving found on the top rails or stretchers, the tops of mirrors, etc.

CROTCH MAHOGANY: Mahogany cut from the fork of the tree to show the decorative grain.

CRUCIFORM: Cross shaped.

CURULE LEG: A leg shaped in an ogee (S) curve, used in pairs joined at the center where they cross.

D

de la SALLE, PHILIPPE (1723-1805): A French fabric designer.

DESSERTE: A Louis XVI sideboard with one or more undershelves.

DIAPER PATTERN: An ornamental pattern repeating a design which covers the surface uniformly.

DIRECTOIRE STYLE: A French furniture style appearing in the transitional period between Louis XVI and the Empire, showing a marked severity in comparison with the ornate furniture of the previous years.

DOS D'ANE DESK: *see* Bureau dos d'ane.

DOSSIER PLAT: The flat back of a chair.

E

EGLOMISE: Decoration on glass, frequently in gold leaf, and painted on the reverse side.

EPERGNE: A silver, glass, or porcelain ornamental centerpiece for a dining table, to be filled with fruit, etc.

ESCUTCHEON: Brass plate surrounding a keyhole.

F

FAUTEUIL: A French upholstered armchair, with the arms left open.

FAUTEUIL DE BUREAU: A French desk armchair, usually with a leather seat cushion.

FAUX-BOIS: Wood painted with a grain to represent some other wood.

FEATHEREDGE BOARD: A board trimmed to fine edges which fit into grooves in other boards.

FERAGHAN RUG: An Oriental rug from Persia, the warp and weft of cotton, the short pile of wool; mostly in the Heratic motif.

FINIAL: An ornamental terminal decoration—acorn, flame, urn, etc.—affixed to the top of a piece of furniture.

FIREBACK: An iron plate set against the back wall of a fireplace to radiate heat and protect the brickwork.

FLAME-STITCH UPHOLSTERY: Fabric woven to simulate flames (pointe d'hongroise), used in the 18th century.

FOLIE: An unfinished building or other structure erected for purely decorative purposes. A pavilion.

FORTUNY PRINT: A fabric originally produced in Venice by a secret printing process which gives cotton cloth the effect of brocade or of damask.

FRUITWOOD: Used for French country furniture—principally pear, and apple woods.

G

GADROON: A curved, ornamental edging used on glass and metal objects, and on wooden furniture.

GAINES, JOHN: An American chairmaker of the 18th century.

GALLOON: A woven braid used for trimming upholstery, draperies, etc.

GARNITURE: A set of ornaments used for decoration, usually on a mantel.

GESSO: A composition of plaster and glue used as applied decoration, particularly on mirrors, which hardens and may then be carved and gilded.

GIRANDOLE: A branched candlestick (or wall appliqué) often combined with a mirror, used in 18th century France.

GOUGE WORK DECORATION: An incised decorative design in wood, made with a gouge.

GRANDMOTHER CLOCK: A diminutive tall or case-clock.

GRISAILLE: Painted in tints of gray.

H

HAMADAN RUG: An Oriental rug made in Hamadan, Persia. Most have compact, all over diaper pattern, with outer band in natural camel's hair.

HERAT RUG: An Oriental rug of Persian classification; medium wool pile.

HOOF FOOT: A cloven hoof, used with a cabriole leg. Also called *pied de biche*.

HORN TUMBLERS: Drinking cups fashioned from animal horns.

HUNT TABLE: A sideboard table with frieze, no drawers, and tall enough to serve standing.

I

IMARI: A style of Japanese pottery and porcelain shipped from the Japanese port of that name, principal colors being blue and a bright red.

J

JACOB, GEORGES (1739-1814): A French furniture designer and maker of high note. One of a family of brothers.

JAPANNING: A finish for wood and metalwork consisting of colored shellac with a raised decoration painted in gold and colors, used during the 18th century.

KAKIEMON: A geometric pattern in color credited to the Japanese potter, Kakiemon, circa 1650.

KAS: A Dutch cupboard.

KASHAN RUG: An Oriental rug woven in Kashan, Persia with a short pile of fine wool or silk. Mostly floral designs.

KERMAN RUG: An Oriental rug from Persia, design usually floral, with central medallion, and special corner borders.

KINGWOOD: From Brazil. Similar to rosewood but lighter in color and with more contrasted markings.

L

LAMBETH DELFT: English faïence made at Lambeth and other London localities from the 17th century to 1763.

LANDSEER, SIR EDWIN H. (1802-73): English painter of animals.

LANTERN: A large type of enclosed lighting fixture suspended from the ceiling.

LAWRENCE, SIR THOMAS (1769-1830): English portrait painter.

LE BRUN, CHARLES (1619-90): Celebrated French decorative artist under Louis XIV.

LEEDS WARE: English pottery manufactured the latter part of the 18th century. Its open work designs placed it in a class by itself.

LIGNUM VITAE: An extremely hard, heavy wood; dark brown streaked with black; from tropical America.

LIT DE REPOS A CROSSE: A daybed with scrolled ends.

LIVERPOOL WARE: 18th century English transfer pottery.

LUSTER WARE: Earthenware which becomes brilliant in the baking process by applying metallic oxides to the glaze.

M

MAJOLICA WARE: A glazed, richly colored and ornamented Italian pottery.

MANCHU YELLOW: A color reserved for objects made for the royal family of China only.

MARLBORO LEG: A square tapering leg terminating in an enlarged square or plinth foot.

MARQUETRY: Veneered woodwork sometimes inlaid in very elaborate designs and in contrasting color with the basic material.

MEISSEN WARE: A high grade decorated porcelain made near Dresden, Germany during the 18th century.

MELON TURNED LEGS: Legs carved in the shape of a melon with vertical markings.

MENUISIER: A French craftsman who works in solid woods as differentiated from those who work with veneers. A carpenter.

MING PERIOD: The Chinese dynasty of 1368-1644, covering the reigns of seventeen Emperors. Noted for its exquisite works of art.

MOCHA WARE: Mottled and banded cream ware. A soft paste pottery made in England and in America.

MONTIGNY, PHILIPPE-CLAUDE (1734-1800): A French cabinetmaker (*ebeniste*) of unusual ability in marquetry.

MOUNTS: Hardware ornaments applied to furniture.

MORAN, THOMAS (1837-1926): American etcher and landscape painter.

N

NEEDLEPOINT: Single stitch work for upholstery. Done in silk it is called *petit-point;* in wool it is *gros-point.*

O

ORMOLU: Decorative brass or other metal mounts, gilded and applied to fine furniture, mirrors, etc.

OUSHAK RUG: A Turkish rug, made in or near Oushak of all-wool. Types include Gulistan, Enile, Yaprak and Sparta.

P

PAD FOOT: A flattened foot with a pad or cushion formed underneath it.

PASTILLE BURNER: Perforated china vessels, often in cottage form, for burning aromatic pastilles to perfume the air.

PATERA: A flat, circular disk, usually ornamented, used as decoration in architecture and on furniture.

PAVILLON: Pavilion.

PEDIMENT, SWAN NECK: A scrolled pediment of opposed S curves, terminating in paterae.

PEKING ENAMELS: Ceramics enamelled at low temperature with compounds of glass tinted with mineral oxides.

PELMET: Decorative fabric hung on a backing above a window.

PEMBROKE TABLE: A small breakfast table with drop leaves, usually with a drawer.

PIED-DE-BICHE: A cloven hoof type of foot.

PILLEMONT, JEAN (1728-1808): A celebrated French painter and engraver. A foremost designer of Gobelin tapestries.

PLINTH: A low base supporting the body of a piece of furniture or an ornament.

POLYCHROME: Multi-colored.

POUDREUSE: A lady's dressing table.

PRIE-DIEU: A prayer chair with a tall back and a low seat.

PUTTI: Figures of nude infants used in decorative sculpture. (Singular: putto.)

R

RANDOLPH, BENJAMIN: Philadelphia cabinetmaker who worked between 1762-92. A skilled carver who made fine Chippendale-style pieces.

RÉGENCE: That period of French furniture between 1715 and 1723 during the reign of the Duke of Orleans when the style became less ornate. Not to be confused with the English Regency style of nearly one hundred years later.

REGENCY PERIOD: An English furniture style with classical motifs predominating, extending from about 1800 to 1820.

REPOUSSÉ-BRASS: Sheet brass into which designs are hammered.

ROCOCO: An elaborate and flamboyant style of decoration evolved from the Baroque during the Régence.

ROSEWOOD: From Brazil and India. A valuable cabinet wood of dark red or purple color when finished. Streaked and variegated. Very hard, even grained, takes a high polish. First used as inlay for veneer on Hepplewhite, Sheraton and American Empire pieces. During the Regency period in England, and the Empire and Early Victorian eras in America, it was used in solid pieces. In China this wood is known as "Hwang Hwa Li."

RUSSELL, JOHN (1744-1806): An English artist.

S

SABOT: Furniture mount. A bronze shoe fitted to the foot of a commode, etc.

SALT GLAZE WARE: A stoneware with glaze produced by throwing salt into the kiln at the height of firing.

SATINWOOD: Used for decorative inlays, veneer panels, and banding on furniture. That from East Indian trees is hard, gold colored, veined and wavy, takes a high polish and is satiny in appearance. That from Florida has an orange tone; while that from the West Indies is reddish, veined with yellow.

SAUSAGE TURNING: Elongated turnings, shaped like a row of sausages.

SCEAUX PORCELAIN: A French ceramic, made at Sceaux (Seine), from 1735-1810.

SCONCE: A bracket candlestick attached to a wall plaque.

SERPENTINE FRONT: In cabinetwork, a curve composed of a convex section in the center and concaved ones at each end.

SÈVRES: A very fine French ceramic made in both soft and hard paste from 1738 to 1804.

SHAGREEN: A variety of untanned leather.

SLEIGH BED: An American Empire style bed of veneered mahogany with headboard and footboard of the same height and rolled outwardly.

SPLINT SEAT: A seat made of thin, flat strips of wood, often hickory, interwoven.

SPADE FOOT: A tapered, rectangular foot.

STRAPWORK: A narrow interwoven band in ornamentation.

SUNBURST: An imitation of the rays of the sun in decoration.

SWAG: A curved festoon attached at each end.

SWASH TURNING: Turnings in which the grooves spiral like a screw thread but much more steeply.

TROMPE L'OEIL: A decoration that deceives the eye, such as an illusionary painting.

TRUMEAU: A French pier mirror; most of them having a carving or painting above the glass.

T

TALL CLOCK: A case or "grandfather's" clock.

TAPIS: Tapestry, or like material used for hangings, table-covers, etc.

TAVERN TABLE: A small table of the Jacobean style—rectangular, oval, octagonal or round, with the top extending widely over a deep apron, which sometimes includes a drawer. A box stretcher is usual, near the floor.

TEAKWOOD: A strong, durable, hard wood from the teak tree of the East Indies. Yellowish brown in color. Widely used for Indian furniture. Contrary to popular belief, teakwood is never found in traditionally Chinese cabinet-work.

TESTER: A bed canopy, supported by the four posts or suspended from the ceiling.

TIGER WARE: A German ceramic of the 16th and 17th centuries. Jugs were elaborately mounted with silver.

TOBY JUG: An English pottery beer jug.

TÔLE: Sheet metal, generally tin, which is painted. Used for sconces, lanterns, oil lamps, etc.

TRENCHER: A flat earthenware plate with a narrow rim.

TRACY WINDSOR: A Connecticut Windsor chair made by Colonel Ebenezer Tracy (1744-1803).

TRICTRAC: The game of backgammon.

TRIDENT: A three pronged spear.

TRIFID FEET: A foot divided into three sections or toes.

TROYE, EDWARD: (1808-84). An American artist who painted horses.

V

VALANCE: Drapery border of a bed canopy, above a window, or hanging from a bed frame to the floor.

VERTU: (or Virtù). A curio or work of fine art.

VITRINE: A display cabinet with glass doors.

VOLUTE: A spiral scroll.

W

WEST, BENJAMIN (1738-1820): An American painter who worked principally in England.

WHATNOT: An open shelved stand for displaying small items.

WHEEL BACK CHAIR: An English made chair designed by Robert Adam with an open back, resembling a spoked wheel.

WHIELDON WARE (1719-95): Pottery made by Thomas Whieldon of Staffordshire, noted for its variety of colored glazes.

WINE COOLER: A container on feet in which bottles of wine might be cooled by ice. Chippendale designed lead lined ones of mahogany.

WOOD, RALPH (1715-72): English Staffordshire potter, noted chiefly for his Toby jugs.

WYETH, ANDREW: A contemporary American artist.

DATE DUE